D0581527

THE USBORNE PICTURE DICTIONARY

Felicity Brooks

Designer and modelmaker: Jo Litchfield

Design and additional illustrations by
Mike Olley and Brian Voakes

Photography by Howard Allman

Contents

Managing Designer: Mary Cartwright
Editorial Assistant: Fiona Patchett
Additional models by Les Pickstock, Barry Jones, Stef Lumley, Karen Krige and Stefan Barnett
With thanks to Staedtler for providing the Fimo® material for models.
Bruder® toys supplied by Euro Toys and Models Ltd.

TED SMART

Using your dictionary

The words in a dictionary are in the same order as the letters of the alphabet. This means words that begin with A come first, then words that begin with B, and so on. In this dictionary there are many things on each page to help you to find the word you are looking for.

This letter in a blue square shows the first letter of the words on that page.

This word shows the first word on the page.

This word shows the last word on the page.

The words that you can look up are shown in blue. You can find out about the words in brackets on page 4.

Don't forget that in a dictionary you read down the page in columns. In most other books you read across.

Sometimes the same word appears twice with little numbers next to it. This shows that the same word can be used in two very different ways.

If you forget the order of the letters in the alphabet, look at the bottom of any page.

The blue letter also shows the first letter of the words on that page.

How to find a word

1 Think of the letter the word starts with. "Stone" starts with an "s", for example.

2 Look through the dictionary until you have found the "s" pages.

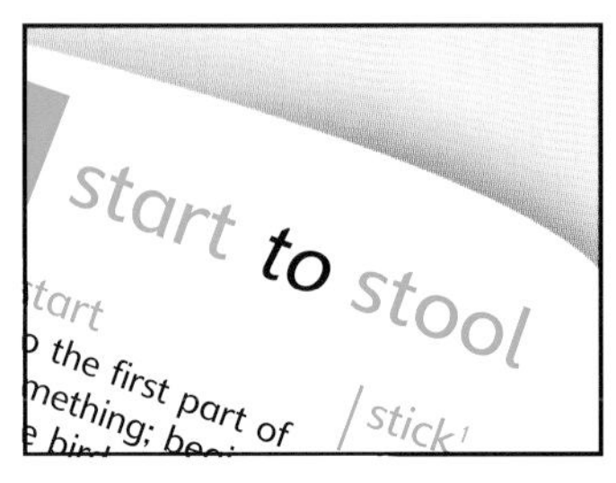

3 Think of the next letter of the word. Look for words that begin with "st".

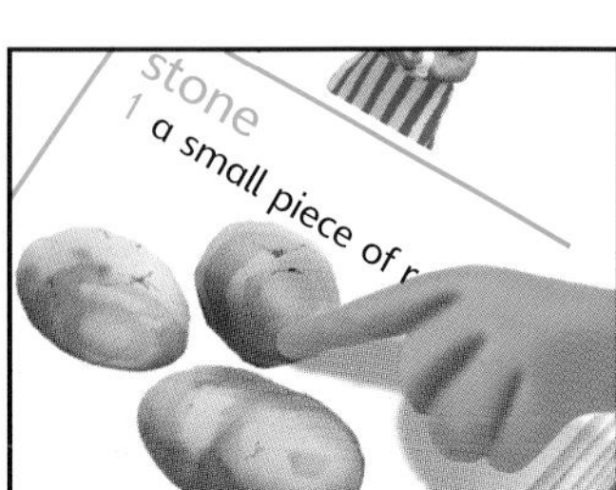

4 Now look down all the "st" words until you find your word.

Can you find?

For practice, you could try looking up these words:

bat
street
lion
hill
wash
jacket
cake
music

Alphabet game

Can you put the names of these fruits in alphabetical order?*

*Answer: apple, banana, cherry, grapes, lemon, pineapple, raspberry, strawberry

Looking at a word

When you have looked up a word, here are some of the things you can find out.

You can find out what a word means.

You can find out how to spell a word.

You can see how you can use a word.

know (knew known)
1 If you know someone, you have met them before.

These children know each other.

2 have something in your mind

You can see if a word can mean different things.

A picture tells you more about a word.

hippopotamus
(also called a hippo)
a very big animal with short legs and thick skin

You can also find out if a word can be shortened.

hen (also called a chicken)
a bird that farmers keep

This tells you another word for the same thing.

Net[2]
a short name for the Internet

You can find out if a word is short for something.

know (knew known)
1 If you know someone, you have met them before.

Turn the page to find out about words in brackets.

Talking about the past

"Doing" words, such as "walk", "smile" and "eat" are called verbs. When you use a verb to talk about the past (the time before now), you usually just add "ed" or "d" to the end of the word:

Danny likes to walk to school.

Yesterday Danny walk**ed** to school.

Danny has walk**ed** to school every day this week.

My baby can smile.

She smile**d** yesterday.

My baby has smile**d** a lot this week.

For some verbs, you don't add "d" or "ed", but another ending to talk about the past. Some verbs change completely:

Robert likes to **eat** pasta.

Yesterday he **ate** pasta.

He has **eaten** pasta every day this week.

In this dictionary, you can see these changes in brackets ( ) after the word:

eat (ate eaten)

Comparing words

"Describing" words, such as "small", "expensive" and "good" are called adjectives. When you use an adjective to compare things, you usually just add "er" or "est" to the end of the word:

A horse is small**er** than an elephant, but a mouse is the small**est**.

For some adjectives, instead of adding "er" or "est", you say "more" or "most" before the word:

A car is **more** expensive than a bicycle.

A truck is the **most** expensive.

You must be **more** careful.

Sara is the **most** careful.

For a very few adjectives, you don't add "er" or "est", or "more" or "most", but change the whole word:

This cake is **good**.

This cake is **better**.

This cake is the **best**.

In this dictionary, you can see these unusual words in brackets ( ) after the word:

good (better best)

More than one

"Naming" words, such as "goat", "sheep", "mouse" and "child" are called nouns. When you use a noun to talk about more than one thing, you usually add an "s" to the end of the word:

one goat two goat**s**

one house two house**s**

If the word already ends with an "s", you add "es" to the end instead:

one cross two cross**es**

For a very few nouns, you don't add an "s" or "es" to the end, but keep the word exactly the same:

one sheep two **sheep**

For a few nouns you add a completely different ending:

one child two child**ren**

For some nouns, you don't change the ending, but you change the whole word:

one mouse two **mice**

one goose two **geese**

In this dictionary, you can see these unusual words in brackets ( ) after the word:

child (children)

Aa actor *to* ambulance

actor
someone who pretends to be another person and acts in a play

afraid
If you are afraid, you think something is scary or bad.

Maddy is afraid of spiders.

air
what we all breathe

A balloon floats in the air.

add
1 find the answer to a sum like this one:

8 + 2 =

2 put something with something else

Billy's adding two blocks.

after
If something happens after something else, it happens later.

Sacha goes after Suki.

alone
not with other people

Katie's alone in the bath.

address
words that show where someone lives

Oliver Muncher
233 Grub Avenue
Noshington
Chowfordshire
CH23 1NN

afternoon
the part of the day after the morning

3 o'clock in the afternoon

alphabet
all the letters you use to write words, put in a special order:

abcdefghijklm
nopqrstuvwxyz

adult
a grown-up person

Minnie's dad is an adult.

age
how old you are

Can you guess Olivia's age?

ambulance
a special van that takes people to hospital

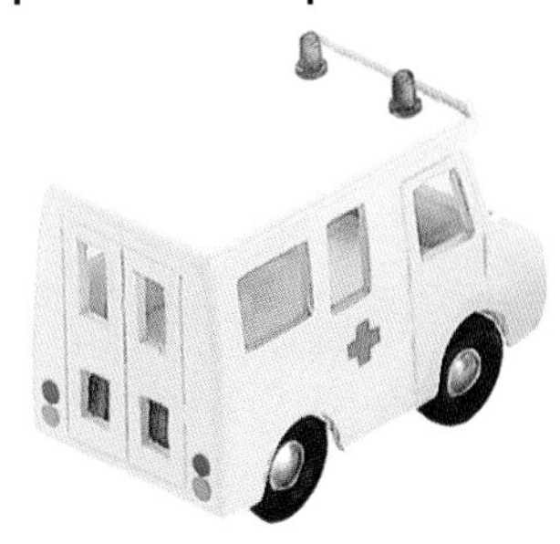

amount
how much there is of something

a large amount of pasta

ankle
the part of your body that joins your leg to your foot

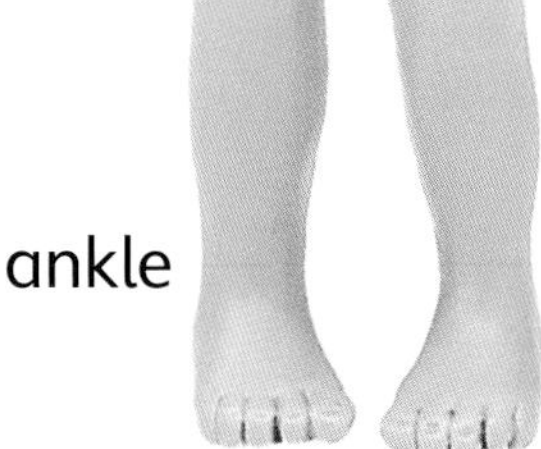
ankle

apple
a round fruit with red, green or yellow skin

angel
a messenger sent from heaven

answer
what you say or write when someone asks you a question

Question: Which animal says "meow"?

Answer: A cat

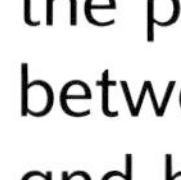

arm
the part of your body between your shoulder and hand

angry
If you are angry, you feel upset and want to shout.

ant
a very small insect

arrive
get to where you are going

The bus has just arrived.

animal
something that lives, moves and breathes

ape
a large animal with long arms and no tail

An orang-utan is an ape.

art
something such as a painting or drawing, that someone has made

Bb baby *to* balance

artist

someone who draws or paints or makes other pieces of art

ask

1 say that you want to know something

2 say that you want something

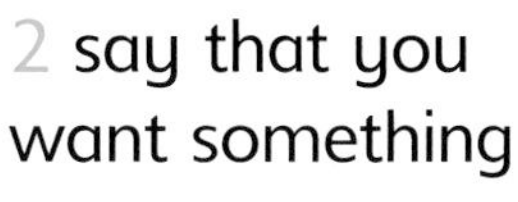

She is asking for strawberries.

asleep

sleeping

astronaut

someone who goes into space

baby

a very young child

back[1]

the part of your body between your neck and bottom

back[2]

the part furthest from the front of something

This boy is sitting at the back of the bus.

bad (worse worst)

1 naughty

a bad dog

2 not good or not good to eat

a bad apple

bag

something you use to hold or carry things

bake

cook food, such as bread or cakes, in an oven

Oliver is going to bake some muffins.

baker

someone who makes and sells bread and cakes

balance

keep your body or something steady so it does not fall

This clown can balance on one hand.

bald
Someone who is bald has no hair on his head.

banana
a long, curved fruit with a yellow skin

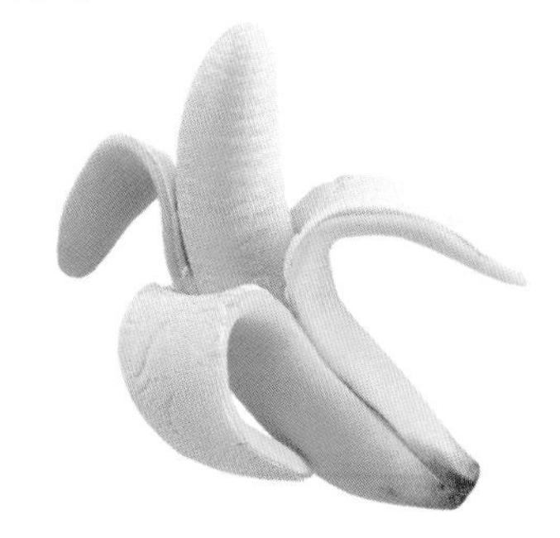

bar
1 a long, thin piece of metal or wood

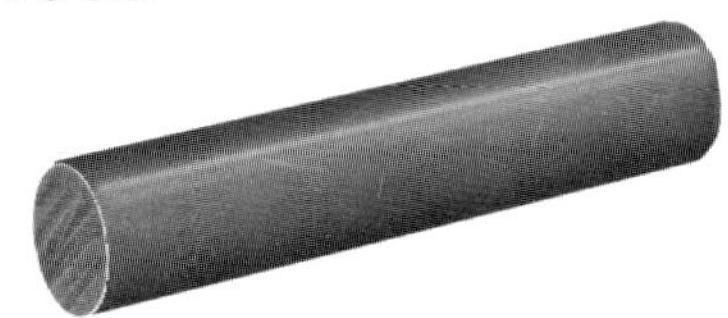

2 a block of something

a bar of soap

ball
1 a round thing that you use for games

2 a big party where people dance

band
a group of people who play music together

bare
If you are bare, you have no clothes on.

ballerina
a woman who does a kind of dancing called ballet

bang
a sudden, loud noise

bark[1]
the hard skin that covers a tree trunk

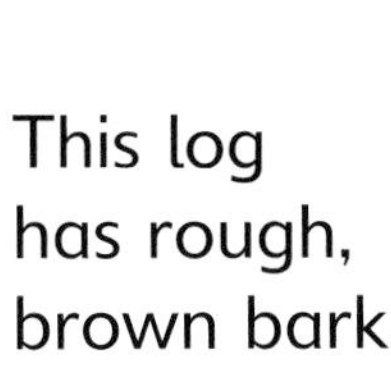

This log has rough, brown bark.

balloon
a thin, rubber bag that gets bigger when you blow into it

bank
1 a place where people keep money safe

2 the edge of a river or stream

bark[2]
When a dog barks, it makes a loud noise in its throat.

barn to bed

barn
a large farm building for animals, straw or machines

base
the bottom part of something

a lamp with a yellow base

basket
something you use to hold or carry things

bat
1 a small, furry animal with wings

2 a kind of stick that you use to hit a ball

bath
something you fill with water and sit in to wash yourself

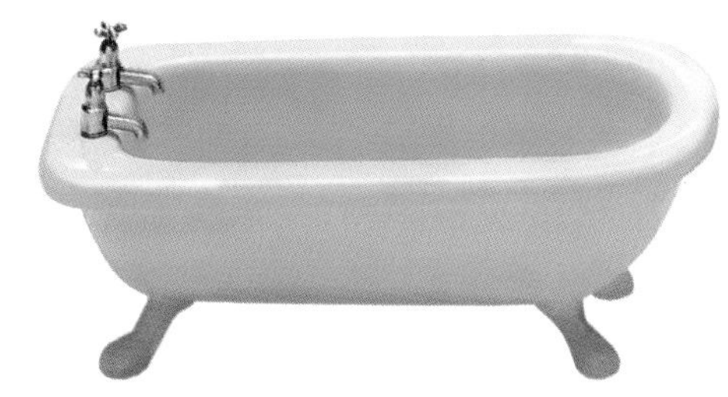

beach
land by the sea with sand or stones on it

playing on the beach

beak
the hard outside part of a bird's mouth

Toucans have big beaks.

bean
a long, thin vegetable, or the seeds inside it

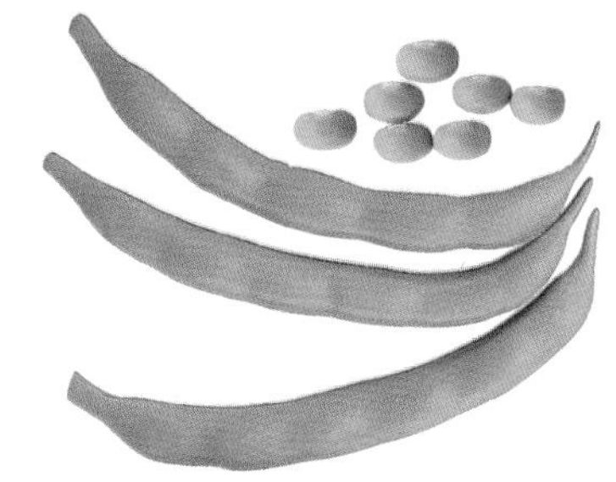

bear
a big, wild animal with thick fur

beard
the hair on a man's chin

beautiful
very nice to look at, listen to or smell

a beautiful cake

bed
something you lie on to sleep or rest

bedroom
a room you sleep in

bee
a yellow and black insect that can fly. Some bees make honey.

beetle
a shiny insect with hard outside wings

beetroot (beetroot)
a round, dark red vegetable

before
If something happens before something else, it happens first.

Suki goes before Sacha.

begin (began begun)
start to do something

Sam began to yawn.

behind
Something that is behind something else is at the back of it.

The kitten is behind the flowerpot.

belong
Something that belongs to you is yours.

The book belongs to Suzie.

below
Something that is below something else is under it or lower than it.

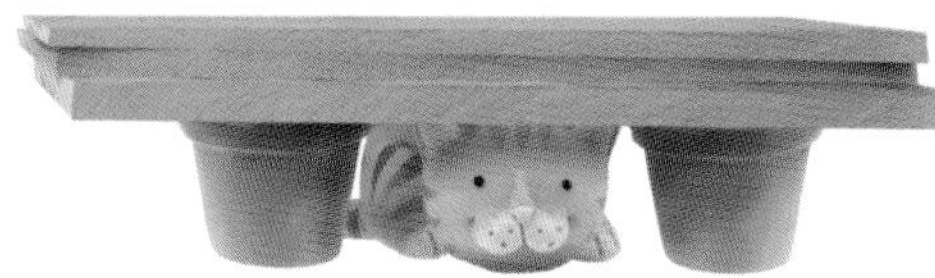

The kitten is below the wood.

belt
a long strip of plastic, leather or cloth that you wear around your tummy

beside
Something that is beside something else is next to it.

The kitten is beside the flowerpot.

between
Something that is between two things is in the middle of them.

The kitten is between the flowerpots.

bib
something that a baby wears around its neck to keep its clothes clean

birthday
the date that you were born

a birthday party

boat
something that floats and can carry people and things across water

bicycle
a machine with two wheels, that you can ride

bite (bit bitten)
use your teeth to cut into something

body
Your body is every part of you.

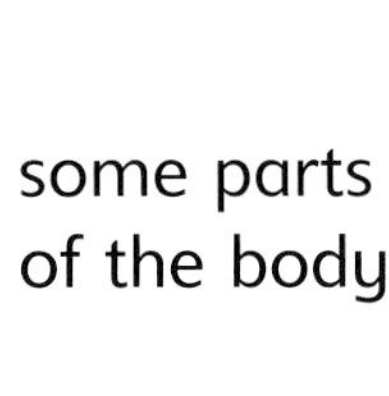

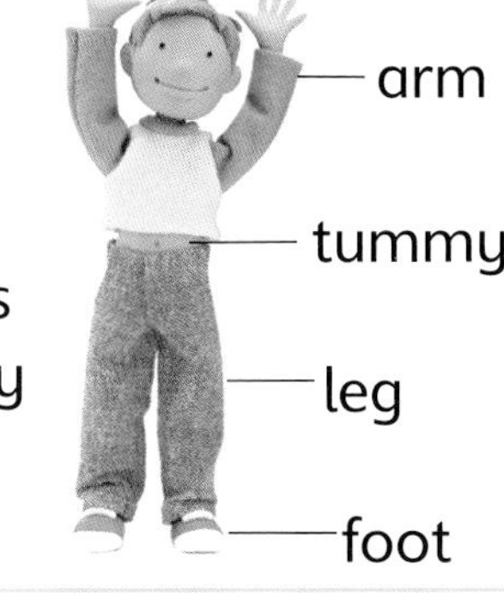

some parts of the body

big
large; not small

a big elephant

blanket
a thick cover that you can put on a bed

bone
the hard, white parts inside your body or inside an animal's body

Patch is gnawing a toy bone.

bird
an animal that has a beak, wings and feathers

blow (blew blown)
1 make air come out of your mouth

2 When the wind blows, it moves the air.

book
something that you read that has pages fixed inside a cover

boot *to* breakfast

boot
a tall shoe that covers your foot and ankle

bowl
a kind of round, deep plate that holds food

brave
not afraid to do something scary

a brave firefighter

bottle
something made of glass or plastic that holds liquids

box
something made of cardboard, wood or plastic that you can keep things in

bread
a food made from flour and baked in an oven

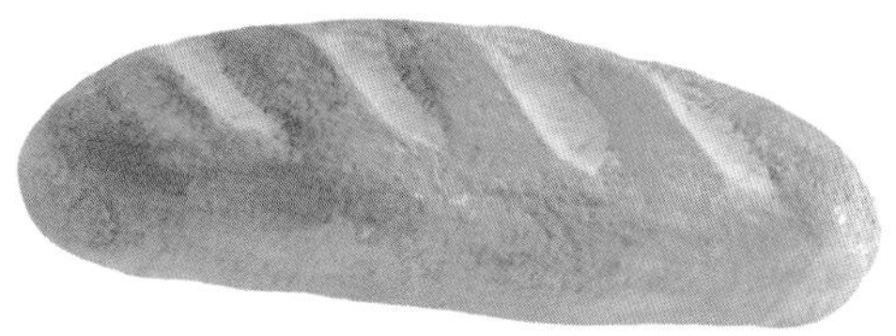

bottom[1]
the part of your body that you sit on

boy
a child who is not a girl

break (broke broken)
make something split into pieces or stop working

bottom[2]
the lowest part of something

The kitten is at the bottom of the stairs.

branch
part of a tree that grows from the trunk

breakfast
the first meal of the day

breakfast foods

breathe *to* burn

breathe
suck air through your nose or mouth and send it out again

Divers carry air to breathe under water.

bridge
something built over a road, river or railway so that people can get across

bright
If a colour or light is bright, it is strong and easy to see.

a bright yellow car

bring (brought brought)
take someone or something with you

Jack brought his letter to post.

brush
something you use to tidy your hair, clean your teeth or for painting or sweeping

bucket
something you use to hold or carry things, such as sand or water

bug
an insect or other very small animal

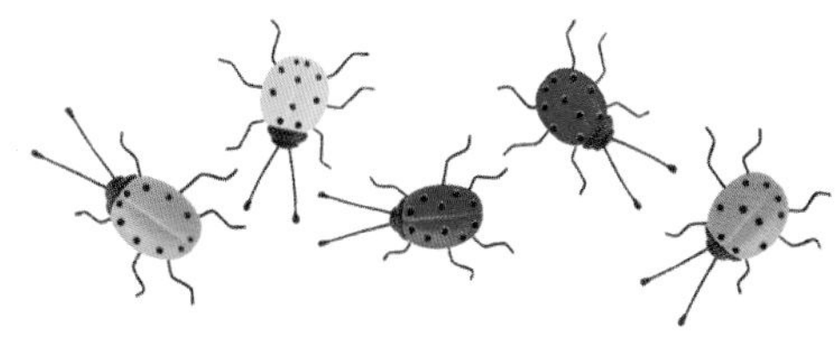

build (built built)
make something by putting parts together

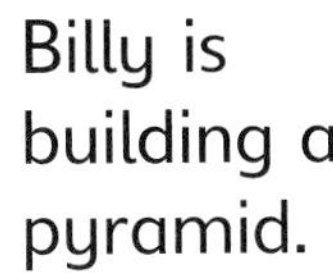

Billy is building a pyramid.

building
a place with walls and a roof

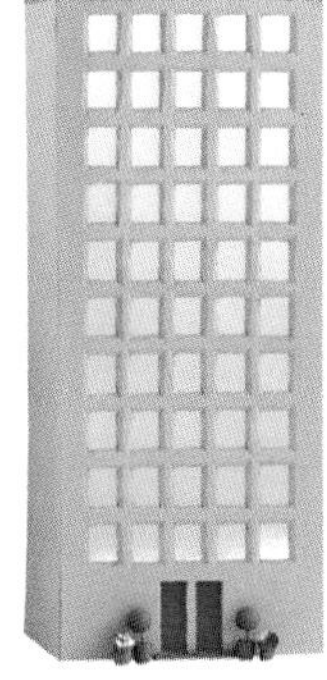

This building has ten floors.

bump
knock something or someone by mistake

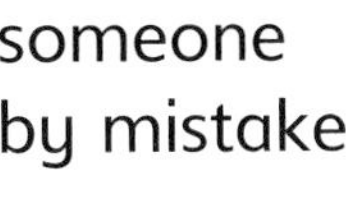

Mr. Bun bumped into a dog.

burger
a round, flat piece of meat that you usually eat in a bun

burn (burnt burnt)
1 ruin or hurt something or someone with fire or heat

Dad burnt the burgers.

2 be on fire

bus
a big thing on wheels that can carry a lot of people

bush
a big plant with lots of branches. Bushes are smaller than trees.

a bush

a tree

busy
If you are busy, you have lots of things to do.

Mr. Bun is busy in the kitchen.

butcher
someone who sells meat

butter
a yellow food made from milk

butterfly
an insect with four large wings

button
a small, round thing that you use to do up clothes

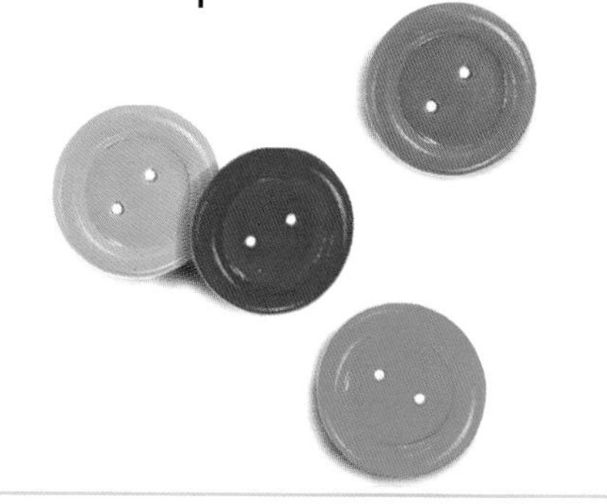

buy (bought bought)
pay money for something so that you can have it

café
a place with tables and chairs where you can buy and eat snacks and drinks

cage
a box or room with bars, for an animal

cake
a sweet, soft food that is baked in an oven

calf
a young cow

a cow and a calf

call to castle

call
1 shout to someone or a pet so that they come to you

2 give someone or something a name

camel
a large animal with one or two humps

camera
something you use to take photographs

camp
live in a tent for a short time

candle
a lump of wax with a string through the middle

cap
a soft hat with a round part at the front that shades your eyes

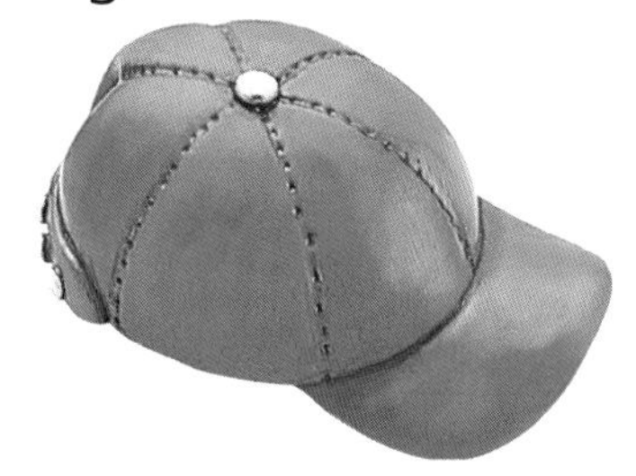

car
a big thing that people drive. It has four wheels and goes on roads.

card
something that you send to people at special times

carpet
a thick cover that is fixed to the floor

This room has a blue carpet.

carrot
a long, orange vegetable

carry
hold something and take it with you

Aggie is carrying some flowers.

castle
a big, strong building with high, stone walls

cat *to* cheap

cat
a furry animal with a long tail

cave
a big hole in a mountain or cliff, or under the ground

There's a bear in this cave.

chair
a seat with a back, made for one person to sit on

catch (caught caught)
1 get hold of something that is moving

Jack caught the ball.

2 get on a bus, train or plane

CD (short for compact disc)
a round piece of plastic with music or information stored on it

chalk
soft white or coloured sticks that you can use for writing and drawing

caterpillar
a small, long animal that will turn into a butterfly or moth

centre
the middle part of something

The fruit is in the centre of the table.

chase
run after a person or animal to try to catch them

Jack and Polly are chasing the dogs.

cauliflower
a big vegetable with green leaves and a white middle

cereal
a kind of food that you eat with milk for breakfast

cheap
not costing much

Everything in this shop is very cheap.

cheese
a food made from milk

chef
someone who cooks the food in a restaurant

cherry
a small, round fruit with a stone in the middle

chick
a very young chicken or other bird

a hen with five chicks

chicken (also called a **hen**)
1 a bird that farmers keep

2 a kind of meat that comes from a chicken

child (children)
a young boy or girl

chin
the part of your face below your mouth

chocolate
a sweet food used to make cakes, sweets and drinks

choose (chose chosen)
pick the things that you want

Billy can't decide which to choose.

city
a very big town where many people live and work

class
a group of people who learn together

classroom
a special room where people have lessons

clean *to* coin

clean[1]
take the dirt off something

close[1] (say "kloze")
shut something

Danny is going to close the door.

clown
someone who wears funny clothes and does tricks to make people laugh

clean[2]
not dirty

The boy in the middle is the only one with clean clothes.

close[2] (say "klose")
near

Bill and Ben are standing close together.

coat
something you wear to keep you warm when you go out

climb
move up or down something high or tall

The firefighter is climbing up the ladder.

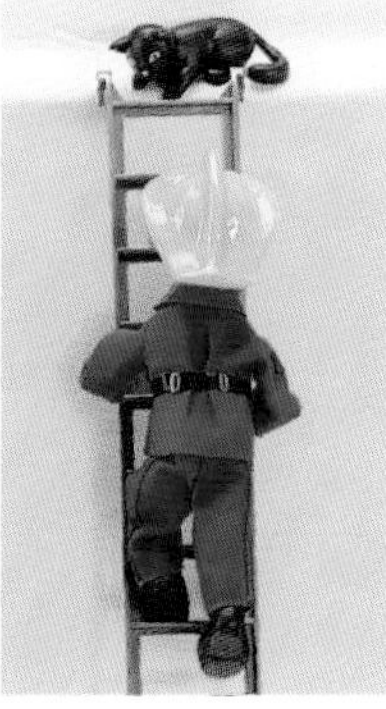

clothes
things that you wear

coffee
a hot, brown drink made from roasted coffee beans

clock
something that shows the time

cloud
white or grey shapes that you see floating in the sky

coin
a small, round piece of metal money

Pete has two coins in his hand.

cold[1]
an illness that makes you cough and sneeze a lot

Helen has a bad cold.

cold[2]
not hot or warm

Sam is wearing gloves because it is cold.

colour
Red, green, yellow and blue are all colours.

comb
something made from metal or plastic that you use to tidy your hair

come (came come)
1 move towards somebody or something

The clown comes into the house.

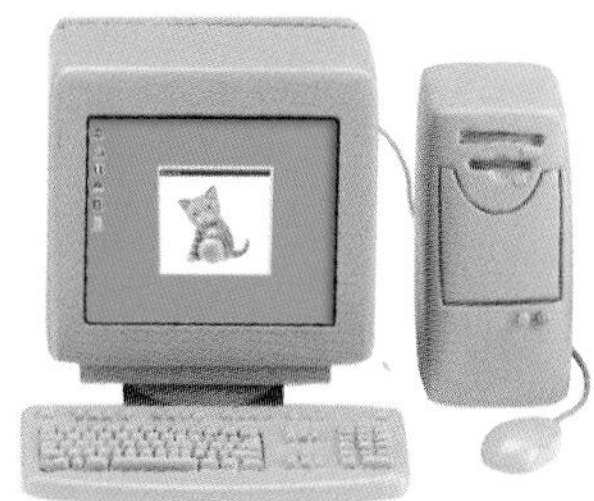

2 arrive
What time does the bus come?

computer
a machine that stores words, pictures and numbers and can send messages

cook
heat food to make it ready to eat

Dad is cooking pancakes.

copy
do the same as someone

Sally is copying Polly.

country[1]
a part of the world with its own name, people and laws

This map shows the countries of Africa.

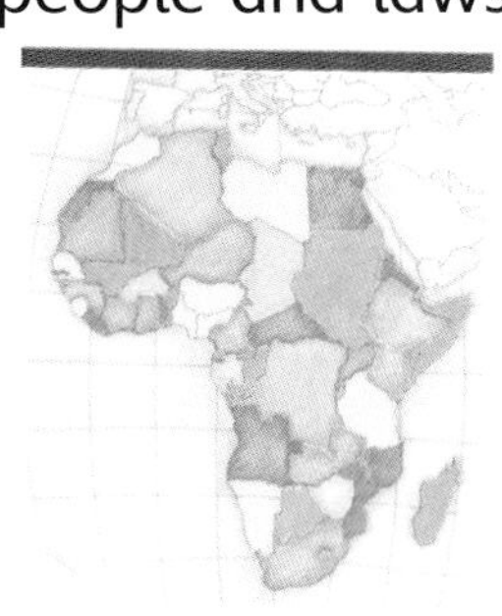

country[2]
the land outside towns and cities

cow
a big farm animal. Most milk comes from cows.

crash
hit something suddenly and make a loud noise

This car has crashed into a tree.

crawl *to* cycle

crawl
move on your hands and knees

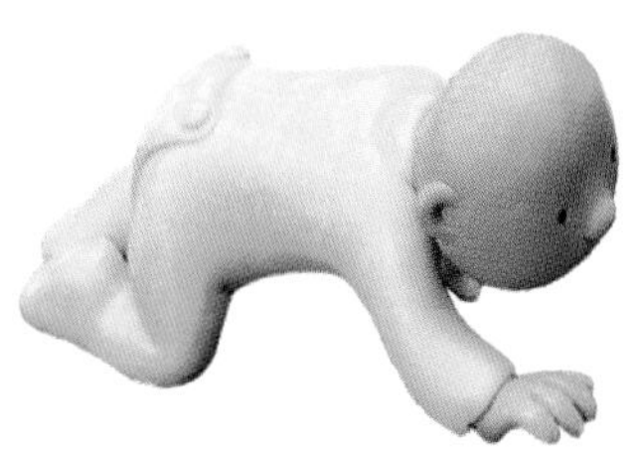

crayon
a coloured pencil or a pencil made from wax

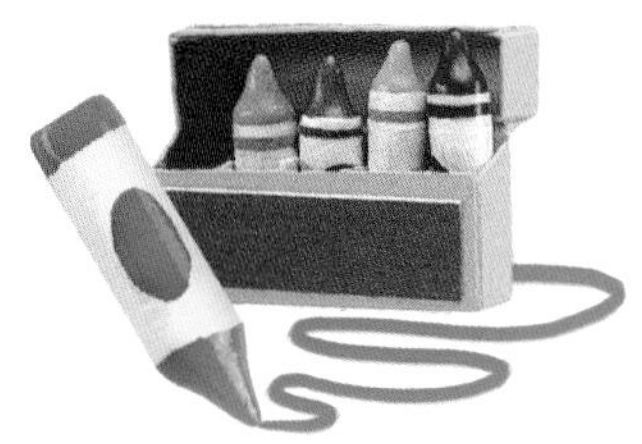

creep (crept crept)
move very quietly and slowly

crocodile
a big animal with sharp teeth and a long tail

cross[1]
a mark made of two lines

cross[2]
go from one side to the other

Danny is crossing the road.

crown
a special gold or silver hat that a king or queen wears

cry
let tears fall from your eyes. You cry when you are hurt or unhappy.

cucumber
a long, green vegetable that you eat in salads

cup
something that you drink from. A cup usually has a handle.

cut (cut cut)
use a knife or scissors to divide something into pieces

cycle
ride a bicycle

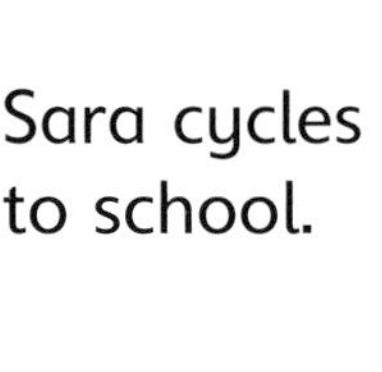

Sara cycles to school.

Dd dance to desk

dance
move your body to music

Steff and Laura are dancing.

dangerous
If something is dangerous, it may kill or hurt you.

Some snakes are dangerous.

dark
1 When it is dark, there is no light.

2 not pale or light

dark blue paint

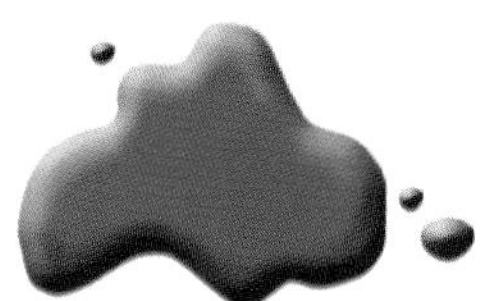

date
the day and month when something happens

What's the date today?

day
1 the time when it is light outside

2 the 24 hours between one midnight and the next

dear
a word that you use at the beginning of a letter

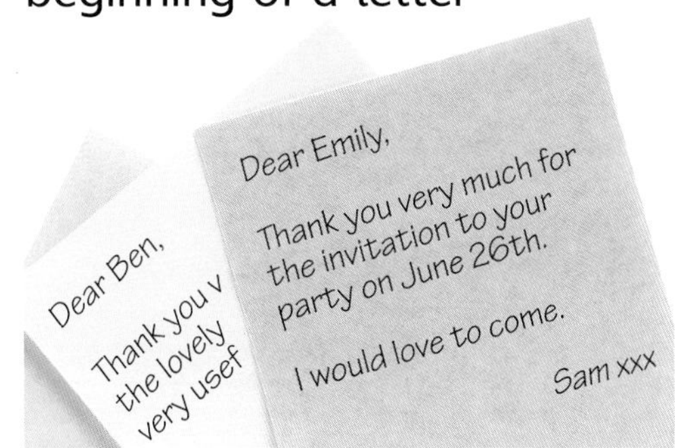

deep
going down a long way

The digger is digging a deep hole.

deer
a big animal that can move quickly. Male deer have big horns called antlers.

delicious
very nice to eat or drink

Jack's sandwich is delicious.

dentist
someone who takes care of your teeth

desert
very dry land where not many plants can grow

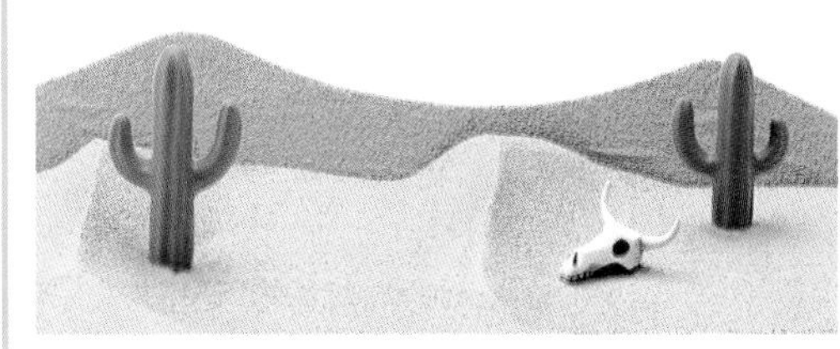

desk
a kind of table that you sit at to read, write or use a computer

dictionary

a book of words. It tells you what words mean and how to spell them.

a picture dictionary

dig (dug dug)

make a hole in the ground

dirty

covered with mud, food or other stains

die

When someone or something dies, they stop living.

I forgot to water my plant and it died.

digger

a big machine that can dig holes and move earth

disappear

If something disappears, you cannot see it any more.

Polly's dog has disappeared.

different

not the same

The twins are wearing different colours.

dinner

a name for the biggest meal of the day

dive

jump into water with your hands and head first

difficult

not easy to do

It's difficult to look after two babies at the same time.

dinosaur

an animal that lived millions of years ago. Some dinosaurs were enormous.

diver

someone who wears special clothes to swim underwater

do (did done)

1 make something happen

Jenny is doing a jigsaw puzzle.

2 finish something

doctor

someone who helps sick people get better

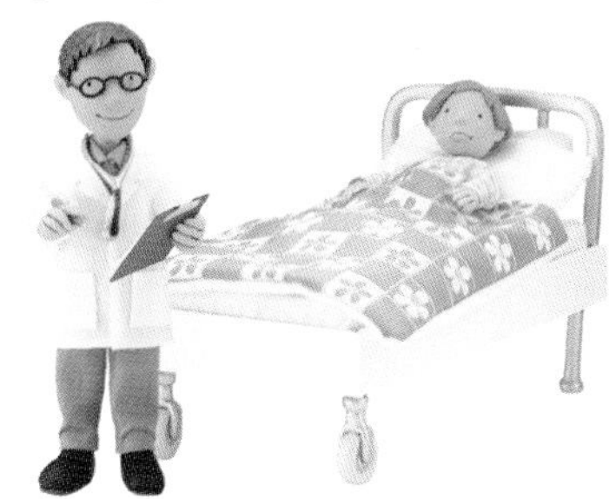

dog

an animal that people keep as a pet or to do work

doll

a toy that looks like a small person

dolphin

a clever animal that lives in the sea. Dolphins are not fish.

donkey

an animal that looks like a small horse with long ears

door

something you use to get into a room, building, car or cupboard

down

from a higher place to a lower one

This arrow points down.

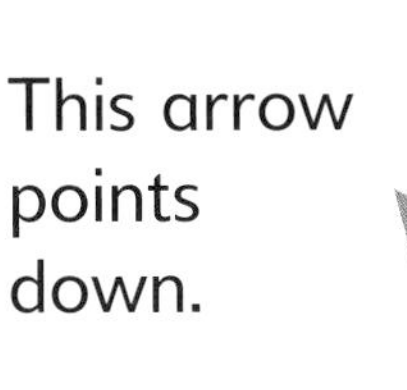

dragon

a monster in stories that has a long tail and wings and breathes out fire

draw (drew drawn)

make a picture with a pen, pencil or crayons

drawing

a picture someone has made with a pen, pencil or crayons

dream

a story that you see and hear while you are sleeping

dress[1]
something that girls and women wear

Anya is wearing a red dress with white flowers.

dress[2]
put on clothes

drink (drank drunk)
swallow water or another liquid because you are thirsty

drive (drove driven)
make a car, bus or other vehicle go somewhere

Mick is driving a dump truck.

drop[1]
a tiny bit of water or another liquid

drop[2]
let something fall

Ellie has dropped her cake.

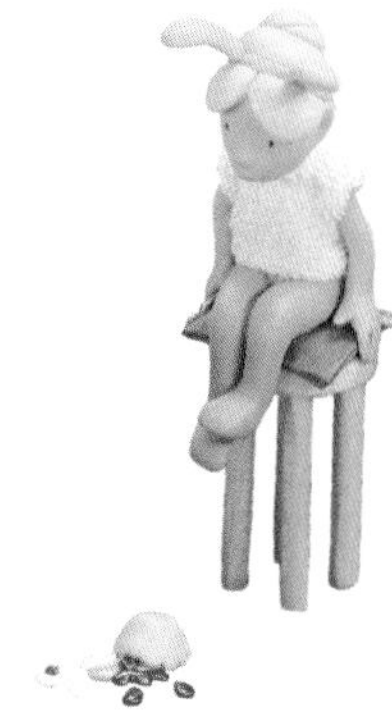

drum
a musical instrument that you hit with sticks or your hands

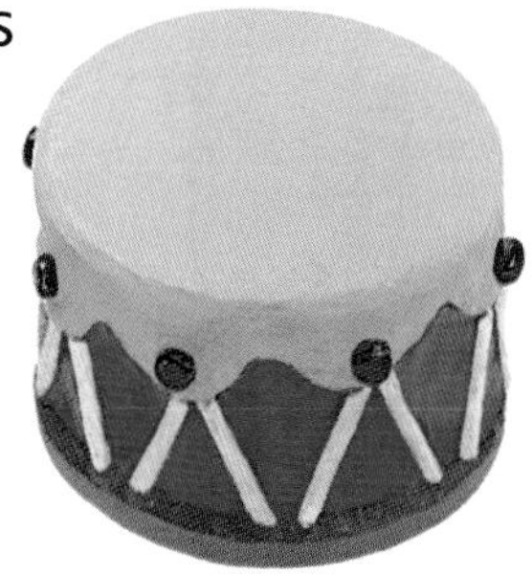

dry[1]
take the water off or out of something or someone

Anna is drying herself with a towel.

dry[2]
not wet or damp

These clothes are dry.

duck
a bird that lives near water and can swim

duckling
a young duck

This duck has three ducklings.

dull
1 not very bright

a dull colour

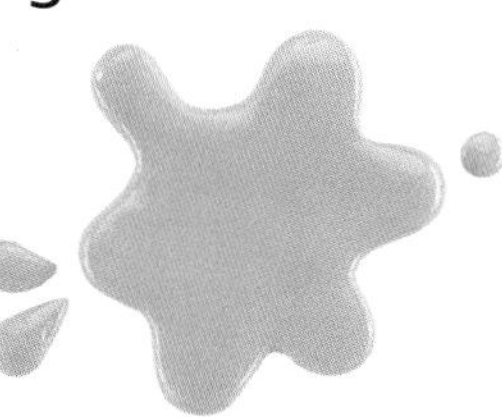

2 not very interesting

a dull story

Ee eagle *to* e-mail

eagle
a big bird with sharp claws and a curved beak

easy
not hard or difficult to do

an easy sum

elbow
one of the two bony parts in the middle of your arms that makes them bend

ear
a part of your body that you use to hear

eat (ate eaten)
put food in your mouth and chew and swallow it

electricity
something that makes lights, televisions, computers and other things work

Electricity comes through wires to make a television work.

early
If you are early, you arrive sooner than someone expected.

Lucy arrived at the party early.

edge
the part along the side or end of something

The crayon is on the edge of the table.

elephant
a very big, grey animal, with a long nose called a trunk

Earth
 the planet that we live on

2 earth
the stuff that plants grow in

egg
a smooth, oval thing that may contain a baby bird, fish or insect.
We often eat hens' eggs.

e-mail
a message that you can send from one computer to another

Polly is sending an e-mail to her friend.

empty
with nothing in it

This jar is empty.

envelope
a paper cover for a letter or card

evening
the part of the day between the afternoon and night

The sun sets in the evening.

end
the last part of something

the end of a TV film

equal
If things are equal, they are the same.

Sally and Amy have equal amounts of sand.

expensive
If something is expensive, it costs a lot of money.

Which toy is more expensive?

enjoy
If you enjoy something, you like doing it.

Molly enjoys singing.

escape
get away from somewhere

Jack's cat escaped from his arms and ran away.

explain
make something clear so other people will understand it

Mr. Levy is explaining how to do these sums.

enormous
very big

Whales are enormous.

even
An even number is a number that you can divide by two.

The bunny is jumping on even numbers.

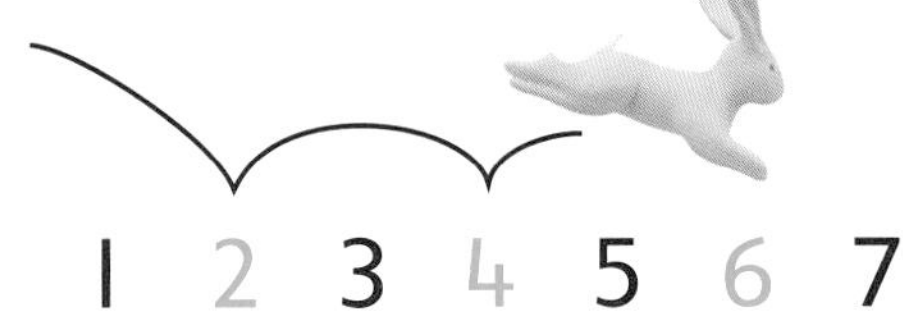

eye
a part of your body that you use to see

face
the front part of your head

a happy face

facing
looking towards someone or something

These giraffes are facing each other.

fact
something that is true

It's a fact that little babies sleep a lot.

fairy
a tiny person, in stories, with wings

fall (fell fallen)
go down to the ground suddenly

The clown fell in a pink pie.

far
a long way

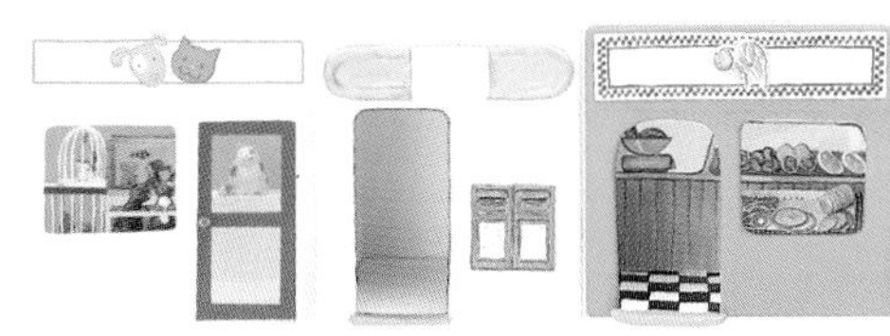

The pet shop isn't far from the butcher's shop.

farm
a place where a farmer keeps animals and grows food

farmer
someone who has a farm

fast
If someone or something is fast, they move very quickly.

Eric can ski very fast.

fat
with a big, round body

a fat cat

feed (fed fed)
give food to a person or animal

feel (felt felt)
1 touch something to find out more about it

2 If you feel happy, for example, that is how you are at the time.

fence
a kind of outdoor wall made from wood or wire

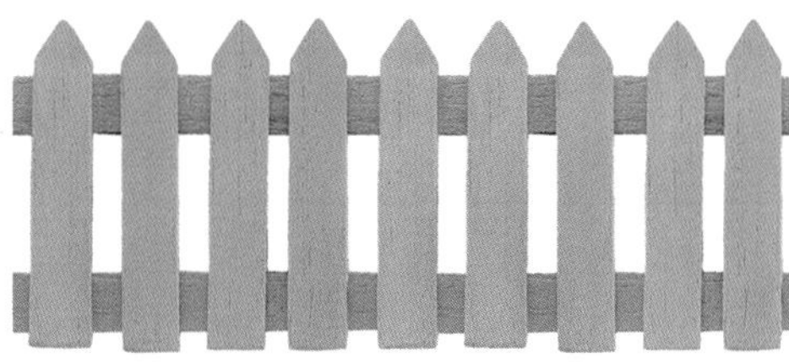

few
not many

Becky only has a few strawberries.

field
a big piece of land where people grow plants or keep animals

fight (fought fought)
When people fight, they try to hurt each other.

The children are playing at fighting.

fill
put so much into something that there is no space for any more

Ivan has filled his wheelbarrow with sand.

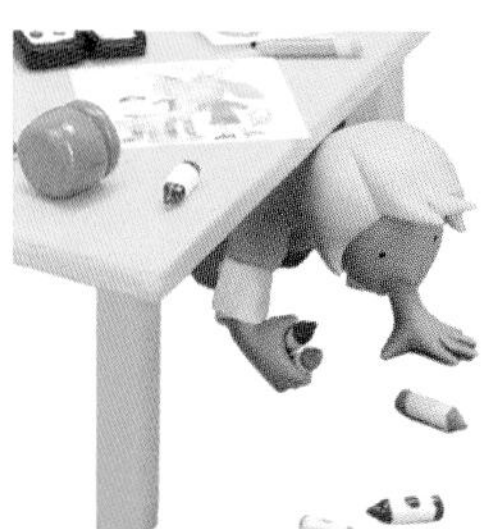

find (found found)
see or get something that has been lost

Megan found the crayons.

finger
one of the five long, thin parts at the end of your hand

finish
come to the end of something

Danny has nearly finished his juice.

fire
heat and bright light that comes from something that is burning

fire engine
a kind of truck that carries all the things firefighters need to put out fires

firefighter
someone whose job is to put out fires

first
before all the others

Jenny is first in the line.

fish to flower

fish[1] (fish)
an animal that lives and breathes under water. We eat some kinds of fish.

fish[2]
use a net or a rod to try to catch fish

fit[1]
If clothes fit you, they are the right size.

Jenny's sweater doesn't fit. It's too big for her.

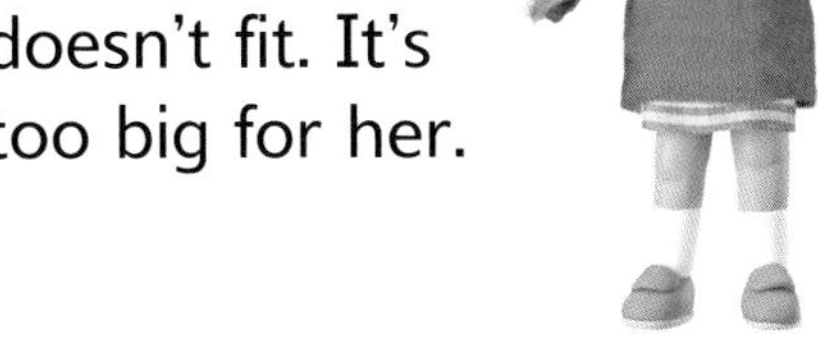

fit[2]
healthy and strong

Alice plays tennis to keep fit.

fix
1 repair something that is broken

Eve is fixing her doll.

2 join something to another thing

flag
a piece of cloth with a special pattern on it. Each country has its own flag.

the French flag

flat
without any curves or bumps in it

Mr. Clack is sawing a flat piece of wood.

float
1 stay on the surface of water

2 stay up in the air

flood
a lot of water that covers ground which is usually dry

floor
the part of a room that you walk on

The floor is covered in toys and clothes.

flour
a powder usually made from wheat that you use to make bread and cakes

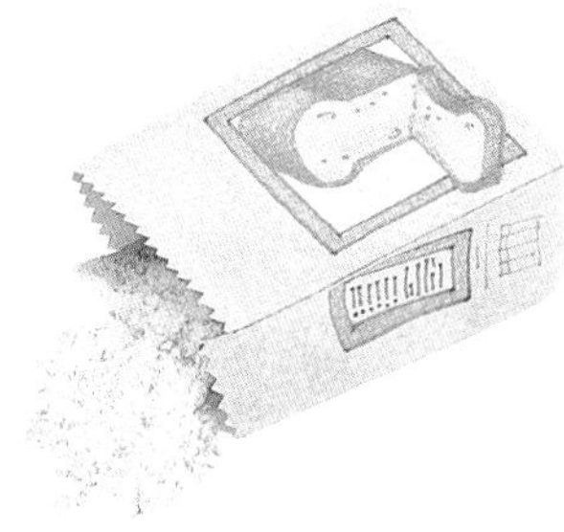

flower
a part of a plant. Flowers are often bright colours.

fly[1]
a small insect with see-through wings

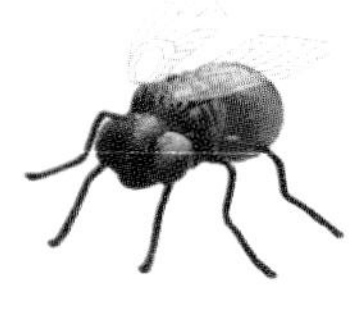

fly[2] **(flew flown)**
move through the air

Birds can fly.

foal
a young horse

a foal a horse

fold
bend one part of something over another part

food
what you eat to stay healthy

foot (feet)
a part of your body at the end of your leg

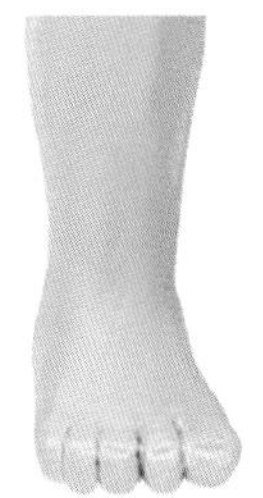

forest
a place where a lot of trees grow close together

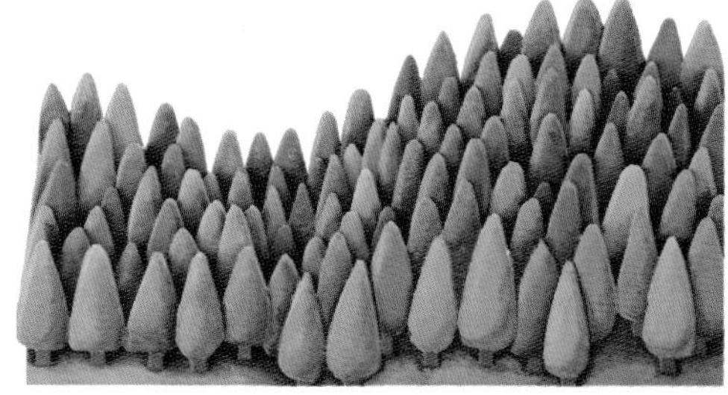

forget (forgot forgotten)
If you forget something, you don't remember it.

Jan has forgotten which way to go.

fork
something that you use to eat with. It has three or four points

fox
a wild animal that looks a bit like a dog. Foxes have long, bushy tails.

free
1 If something is free, you don't have to pay for it.

2 allowed to go where you want or do what you want

freeze (froze frozen)
become very cold

When water freezes, it turns into ice.

freezer
a machine that keeps food very cold so that it does not go bad

fresh
1 If food is fresh, it has just been made or picked and is not bad.

Mrs. Martin sells fresh fruit.

2 If air is fresh, it is clean.

friend
someone that you like and who likes you

Ellie's friends are coming to her party.

friendly
If you are friendly, you like to meet other people and are kind to them.

Marco is very friendly.

frog
a small animal that lives near water. It has big back legs for jumping.

front
the part that comes first or that you see first

front door of a car

fruit
something such as an apple or orange that grows on a bush or tree

fry
cook something in oil or butter

Dad is frying some eggs.

full
If something is full, it cannot hold any more.

Greg's trolley is full of shopping.

fun
If something is fun, you enjoy it and it makes you happy.

Ben and Suki are having fun on the roundabout.

funny
If something is funny, it makes you laugh.

Polly and Jack are laughing at a funny joke.

fur
the soft hair that covers some animals

a cat with soft, white fur

Gg game *to* give

game
something that you play, such as basketball or snakes and ladders. Games often have rules.

gentle
If you are gentle, you are careful, quiet and kind.

Pip is a gentle dog.

gift
something special that you give to someone or that they give to you

garden
a piece of land near a house, where people grow vegetables and flowers

gerbil
a small, furry animal with long legs. Some people keep gerbils as pets.

giraffe
an African animal that has a very long neck and legs

gas
something that is not solid or liquid, and is very light and invisible like air

This balloon is filled with a gas called helium.

ghost
a person who has died that some people think they can see

girl
a child who is not a boy

gate
a kind of door in a fence, wall or hedge

giant
a very tall person, in a story

give (gave given)
let someone have something to keep

Ethan is giving Jenny four wagons for her train.

glad
pleased and happy

Sally is very glad to see her friend.

glass
1 something hard and clear that windows are made from

2 a kind of cup that is made from glass

glasses
something that you can wear on your face to help you see better

glove
something that you wear on your hand to keep it warm

glue
a thick liquid that you use to stick things together

Danny is sticking down paper shapes with glue.

go (went been)
move or travel from one place to another

These cars are going onto the ship.

goal
when you kick, hit or throw a ball into a net, in games such as soccer

goat
a farm animal with a short tail

gold
a yellow metal that is very expensive

good (better best)
1 If something is good, you like it.

2 done well

good work

3+3=6 ✓
2+5=7 ✓
8-6=2 ✓
4+1=5 ✓

3 not naughty

goodbye
a word you say when you go away or someone goes away from you

goose (geese)
a large bird with a long neck

grape
a small, soft purple or green fruit that grows in bunches

a bunch of grapes

grapefruit
a large, round fruit with a thick yellow or pink skin

grass
a plant with thin, green leaves. Grass grows in fields and gardens.

great
1 big or important

2 very good

We had a great day at the beach.

ground
what you walk on outside

Polly is looking at some ants on the ground.

group
a number of people or things that are together

a group of children

grow (grew grown)
get bigger

My plant grew very fast.

grown-up
someone who is not a child

Grown-ups are always chatting.

guess
try to think of an answer to something that you do not know

Can you guess what's in the box?

guest
someone who comes to visit or stay for a short time

Ellie is welcoming her guests to her party.

guinea pig
a small, furry animal that doesn't have a tail

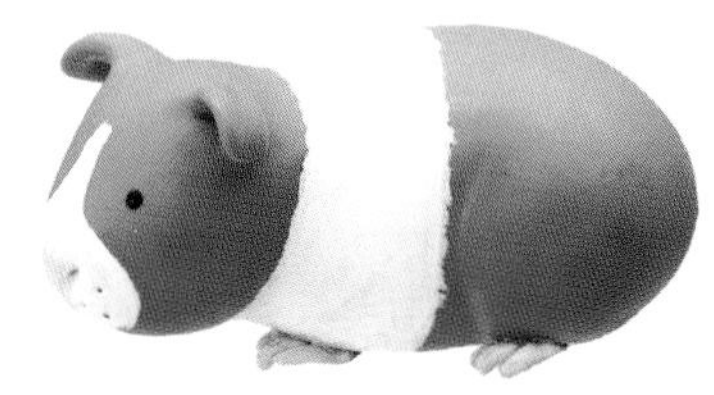

guitar
a musical instrument with strings

hair

the stuff that grows on your head

Rosie has long hair. Katie has curly hair.

hairbrush

something you use to tidy your hair

half (halves)

one of two pieces of something that are exactly the same size

Each mouse has half of the bagel.

hamburger

a round, flat piece of meat that you usually eat in a bun

hammer

a tool that you use for knocking nails into something

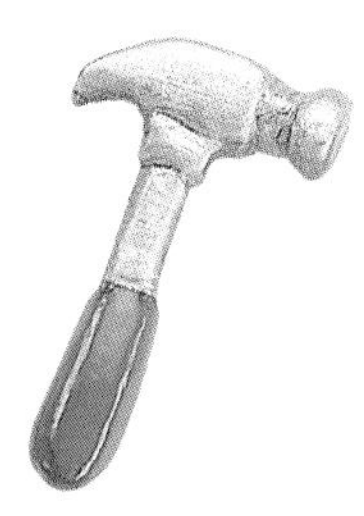

hamster

a small, furry animal with a short tail

hand

a part of your body at the end of your arm

handle

something you use to hold or move something

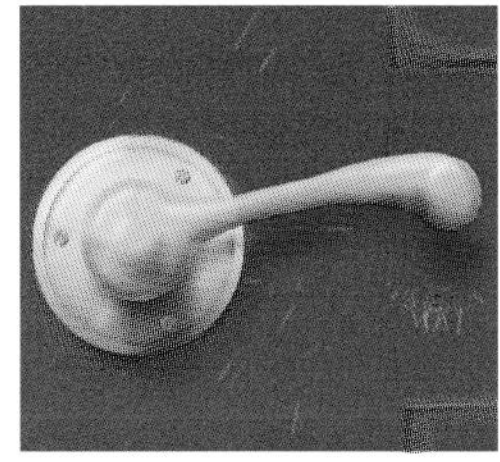

a door handle

hang (hung hung)

put something on a hook, nail or knob

Jack is hanging his coat on a hook.

happen

take place

What is happening in this picture?

happy

If you are happy, you feel pleased about something and not sad.

Sally is feeling very happy today.

hard

1 solid and not soft
2 not easy; difficult

It's hard to put up a tent on hard ground.

hat
something that you wear on your head

hate
If you hate something, you do not like it at all.

Maddy hates spiders.

have (had had)
1 If you have something, it is with you.

Julia has some new red shoes.

2 feel or suffer

Helen has a cold.

head
the part of your body that has your eyes, mouth and ears in it

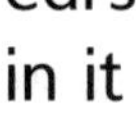

hear (heard heard)
take in sounds through your ears

Jack can hear a dog barking.

heart
1 the thing that pushes blood around your body

My heart is beating fast.

2 a shape

heat
make something hot

Yvonne is heating coffee in the microwave.

heavy
hard to lift, push or pull; not light

Thomas and Jack are trying to move a heavy parcel.

height
how tall someone or something is

Dad is checking Milo's height on the chart.

helicopter
a machine that flies. It has blades on top that spin around very fast.

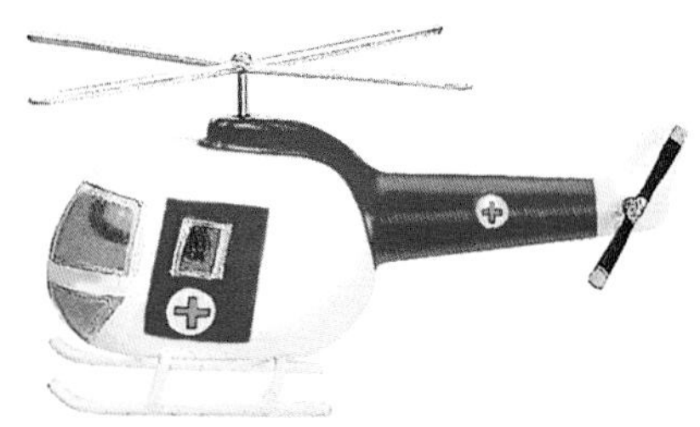

hello
a word you say when you meet someone

helmet
a hard hat that stops you from hurting your head

Grace wears a helmet for skateboarding.

help
do something useful for someone

Jack is helping his dad with the cooking.

hen (also called a chicken)
a bird that farmers keep

hide (hid hidden)
1 go to a place where no one can see you

The clown is hiding from Annie.

2 put something in a place where no one can find it

high
1 a long way from the ground

The balloon is high in the sky.

2 going up a long way

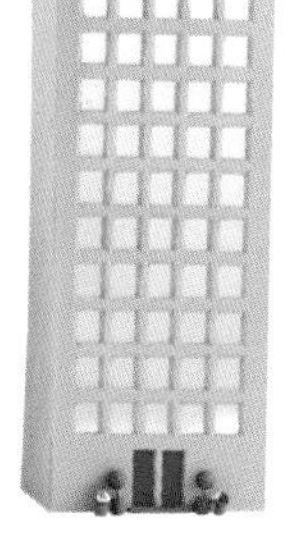

highchair
a special chair for babies and small children

hill
a high piece of land. Hills are not as tall as mountains.

hippopotamus
(also called a hippo)
a very big animal with short legs and thick skin

hit (hit hit)
push or knock someone or something very hard

Alice is hitting the ball with her racket.

hold (held held)
1 have something in your arms or hands

2 have room for something

How many does this hold?

hole
a gap or hollow space in something

There is a hole in this sweater.

home
the place where you live

honey
a sweet, sticky liquid that bees make

hop
jump on one leg

horse
a big animal with four legs and a long tail. People ride horses.

hospital
a building where you go when you are ill or hurt. Doctors and nurses work in hospitals.

hot
very warm; not cold

Don't touch the hot saucepans!

hotdog
a special kind of sausage that you eat in a long, soft bread roll, with mustard

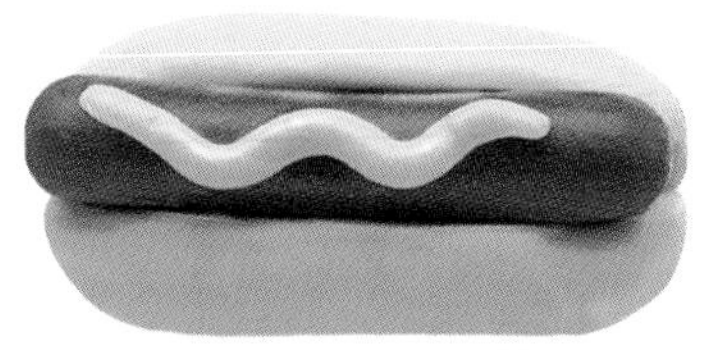

hotel
a big building with a lot of bedrooms. You can pay to stay there.

HOTEL LUCIDA

hour
an amount of time. There are 60 mintues in an hour and 24 hours in a day.

On a clock, the little hand shows the hours.

house
a building that people live in

hug
put your arms around someone or something and hold them tightly

hungry
If you are hungry, you want to eat something.

Oliver is very hungry.

hurry
do something fast

Jack and Polly are hurrying to catch a bus.

hurt (hurt hurt)
If something hurts, you feel pain there.

Ross is crying because his tummy hurts.

ice
water that has frozen solid

ice cubes

ice cream
a very cold, sweet food made from cream or milk

idea
something new that you think of

Andy has an idea.

insect
a small animal with six legs

inside
1 in something

This kitten is inside a flowerpot.

2 in a building; indoors

instead
in place of something

Internet
millions of computers all over the world linked together. You can use the Internet to find out things.

Polly is using the Internet.

invitation
something that you give to someone to ask them to do something with you

invite
ask someone to come somewhere or do something

iron
something you use to make your clothes smooth.

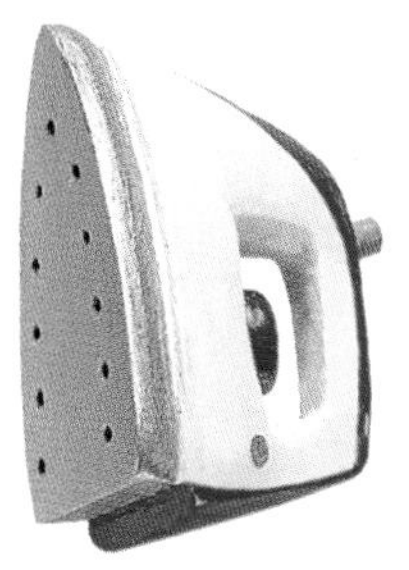

island
a piece of land with water all around it

itch
If your skin itches, you want to scratch it.

George's ear itches.

Jj jacket *to* jungle

jacket
a short coat

Kathy is wearing a yellow jacket.

job
1 what someone does to earn money

Aggie has a job as a gardener.

2 something that needs to be done

juggle
keep two or more things in the air by throwing and catching them, one after the other

jar
something that you keep things in. Jars are usually made of glass.

join
1 become part of a club or group

2 fix two things together

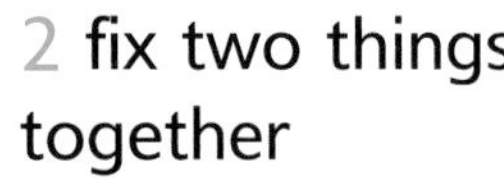

Ethan's going to join the wagons to the train.

juice
liquid that comes from fruit or vegetables

jeans
trousers made from a strong material called denim

joke
something you say to make people laugh

jump
use your legs to push yourself suddenly into the air

jigsaw
a picture cut into pieces. You put the pieces together to make the picture again.

journey
If you go on a journey, you travel from one place to another.

a train journey

jungle
a place in a hot country where many trees and plants grow and many animals live

Kk kangaroo *to* kite

kangaroo
a large animal that moves around by jumping

keep (kept kept)
1 have something and not give it away

Sam keeps his things on a shelf.

2 make something stay the same

key
something you use to unlock a door or to start a car

kick
hit something with your foot

kid
1 a child

2 a young goat

a goat and a kid

kill
make something die

Someone has killed my plant.

kind[1]
a type or sort

There are lots of different kinds of fruit.

kind[2]
If you are kind, you help other people.

Mr. Dot is kind. He does all his neighbour's shopping.

king
a man who rules a country. Kings come from royal families. They are not chosen.

Adam is dressed up as a king.

kiss
touch someone with your lips

kitchen
a room where you make meals

kite
a toy that flies in the wind on the end of a long string

kitten
a young cat

This kitten is playing with a ball of wool.

knee
the bony part in the middle of your leg that makes it bend

kneel (knelt knelt)
get down on your knees

knife (knives)
something you use to cut things. It has a long, sharp edge and a handle.

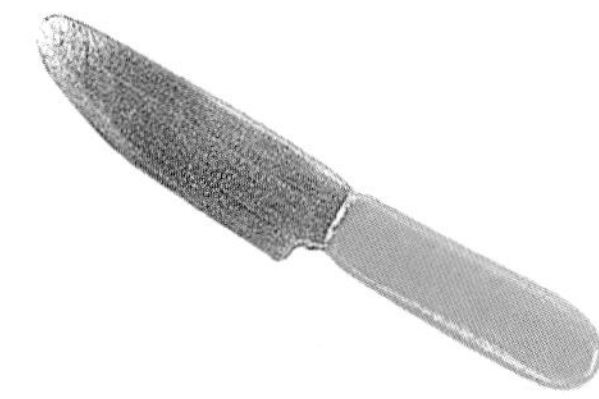

knight
a soldier who lived a long time ago. Knights wore armour and rode horses.

knock
hit something hard

Pip knocked the chair over.

knot
a place where something, such as string, is tied

know (knew known)
1 If you know someone, you have met them before.

These children know each other.

2 have something in your mind

ladder
something you can use to climb up to high places

lady
a woman

These ladies are chatting.

ladybird
a small red or yellow insect with black spots

lake
a big area of water with land around it

lamb to lean

lamb
a young sheep

a sheep and a lamb

lamp
something that makes light

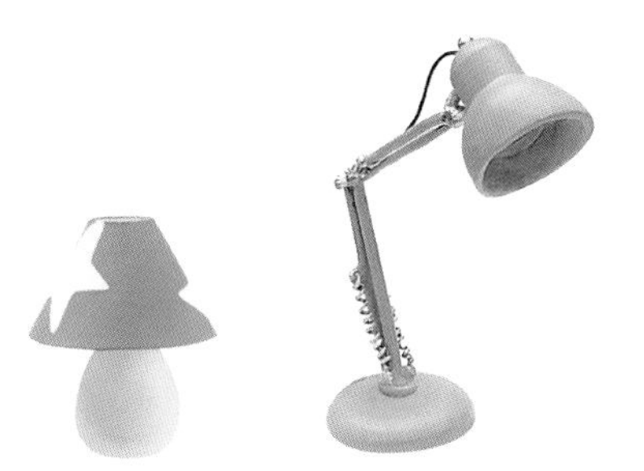

land
the parts of the Earth that are not covered by water

This map shows the land in brown.

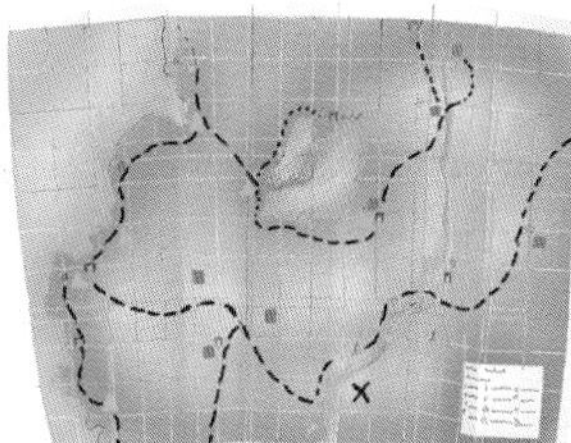

language
the words that people use to speak and write

Alex and Polly are speaking different languages.

large
If someone or something is large, they are big.

Becky is standing under a large tree.

last
1 at the end

The black dog is last.

2 the time before

late
1 after the right time

The bus is late again.

2 near the end of something

laugh
make sounds that show that you think something is funny

lazy
If a person or an animal is lazy, they do not want to do anything.

a lazy cat

lead (led led)
go in front to show the way

This duck is leading her ducklings.

leaf (leaves)
one of the thin, flat parts of a plant or tree

lean (leant leant)
bend to one side

the Leaning Tower of Pisa

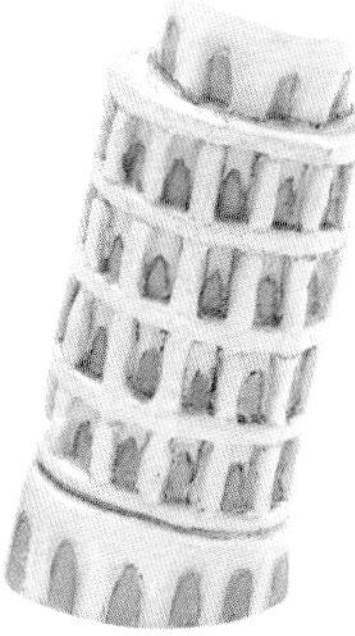

learn (learnt learnt)
get to know and understand something you did not know before

Steve is learning to play the guitar.

leave (left left)
1 go away from a place

Mr. Bun is leaving.

2 let something stay where it is

I left my bag at home.

left
on the side opposite the right side

Lisa is holding the crayon in her left hand.

leg
a part of your body that you use for standing and walking

Tamsin wears tights on her legs.

lemon
a yellow fruit with a thick skin

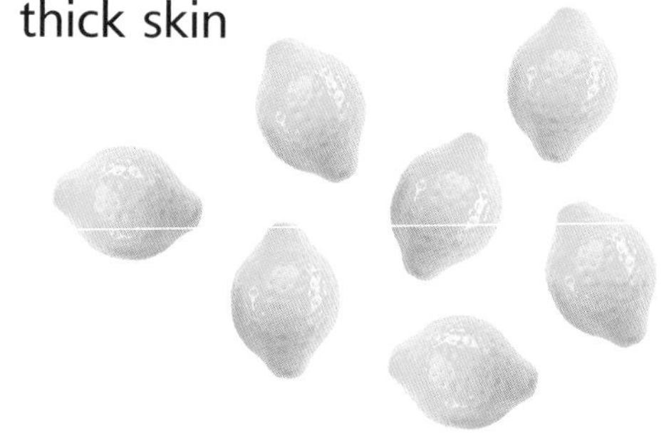

length
how long something is

Use a ruler to measure the length of the paper.

less
not as much

Ethan has less ice cream than Olivia.

lesson
the time when someone teaches you something

let (let let)
If someone lets you do something, they say that you can do it.

Mr. Dot let Jack post his letter.

letter
1 something like A, B or Z that you use to make words

2 a message that you write on paper

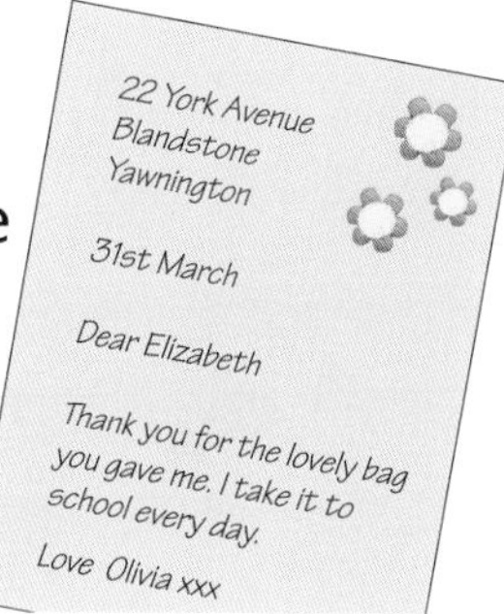

22 York Avenue
Blandstone
Yawnington

31st March

Dear Elizabeth

Thank you for the lovely bag you gave me. I take it to school every day.

Love Olivia xxx

lettuce
a vegetable with big leaves that you eat in salads

lick
move your tongue across something

lid
the top of something like a box or jar

lie[1] (lay lain)
rest with your body flat on something like a bed

lie[2]
say something that is not true

life (lives)
the time when someone or something is alive

Granny and Granddad have had long and happy lives.

lift
pick something up

The clown is lifting a tree out of his bag.

light[1]
1 Light comes from the Sun and from lamps. It lets you see.

2 something that gives light, such as a lamp

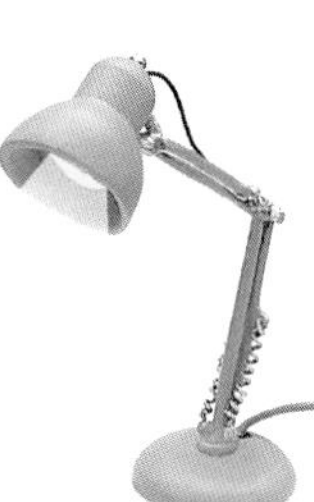

light[2]
1 easy to lift, push or pull; not heavy

2 If a colour is light, it is pale and not dark.

light pink

like[1]
If you like something or someone, you think they are nice.

Becky likes strawberries.

like[2]
If someone is like another person, they are the same in some way.

Sarah looks a lot like her brother.

line
1 a long, thin mark

2 a group of people or things in a row

a line of footballers

lion
a big, wild animal with light brown fur

lip
the edge of your mouth

list to lunch

list
words that someone has written down one after the other

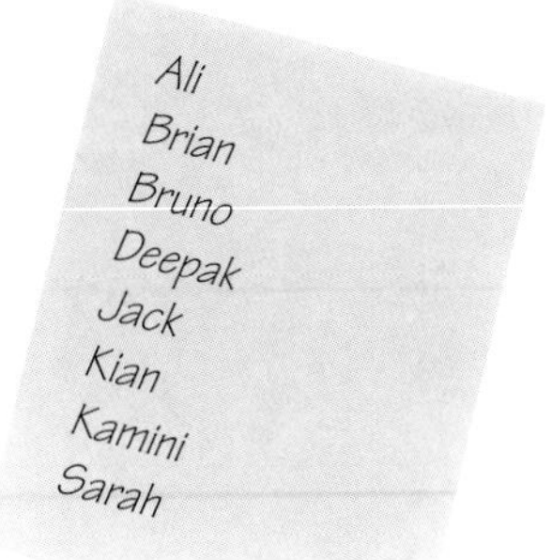

live
1 If you live in a place, that is where your home is.

2 If someone or something lives, they are alive.

lock
something that keeps things like doors and boxes shut. You need a key to open a lock.

a lock

log
a big piece of wood that has been cut from a tree

long
1 If something is long, one of its ends is far from the other.

A giraffe has a long neck.

2 lasting a lot of time

look
use your eyes to see something

Polly is looking at the clown.

lose (lost lost)
1 If you lose something, you can't find it.

2 If you lose a game, you don't win it.

Simon and Ian lost.

lot
a large amount or number

a lot of teddies

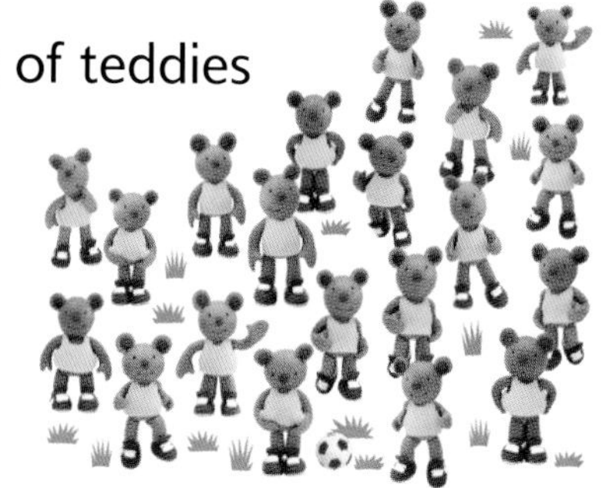

loud
If someone or something is loud, they make a lot of noise.

Steve's guitar is very loud.

love
like someone or something very much

Beth loves having a bath.

low
not far from the ground

This bird is flying very low.

lunch
the meal you eat in the middle of the day

Sally is eating pizza for lunch.

machine
something with moving parts that work together to do a job

a sewing machine

magic
1 In stories, people use magic to make impossible things happen.

2 clever tricks that look impossible

The clown is doing some magic.

main
the biggest or most important

the main entrance of the museum

make (made made)
1 put something together

Ethan is making potato people.

2 If you make something happen, it happens because of something you do.

man (men)
a grown-up who is not a woman

Our teacher is a man.

many (more most)
a large number; a lot of

There are many bees on this flower.

map
a drawing that shows where places are. Maps show roads, rivers and buildings.

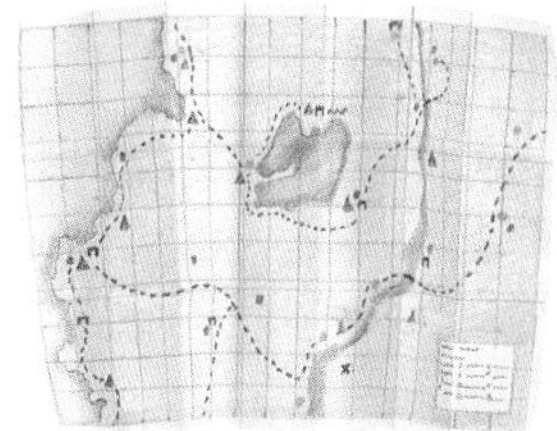

market
a place where you can buy things. Markets are often outdoors.

match[1]
1 a game that two teams play against each other

a football match

2 a small stick that makes fire when you rub its tip against its box

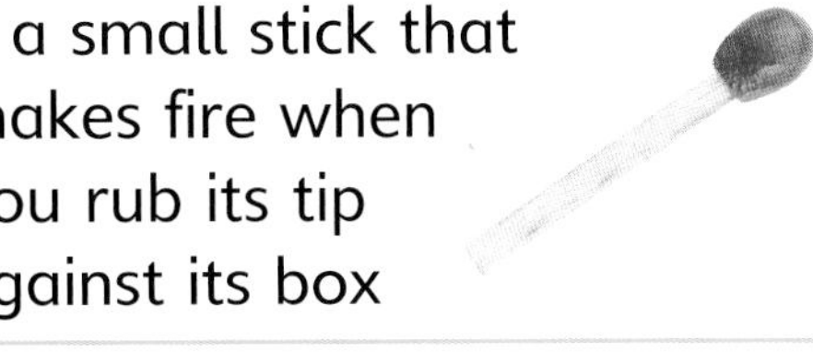

match[2]
If things match, they are like each other in some way.

These socks match.

These socks don't match.

matter
If something matters, it is important to you.

Winning really matters to Neil and his team.

meal
the food that you eat at special times of the day. Breakfast, lunch and dinner are meals.

mean (meant meant)

1 If you say what something means, you explain it.

This means that two groups of two equals four.

2 x 2 = 4

2 plan to do something

measure

find out how big or heavy something is

meat

a kind of food that comes from animals

medicine

liquid that you take when you are ill to make you better

meet (met met)

If you meet someone, you both go to the same place at the same time.

Polly and Lisa met at the fruit stall.

mend

repair something that is broken

Robert is mending his shirt.

mess

untidy and sometimes dirty

What a mess!

message

words that you send or leave for someone when you can't speak to them

Mum!
Paula phoned about tomorrow.
Call her back.

metal

hard stuff that comes out of the ground. Gold, silver, iron and copper are metals.

This bucket is made of metal.

microwave

a small oven that cooks or heats up food very fast

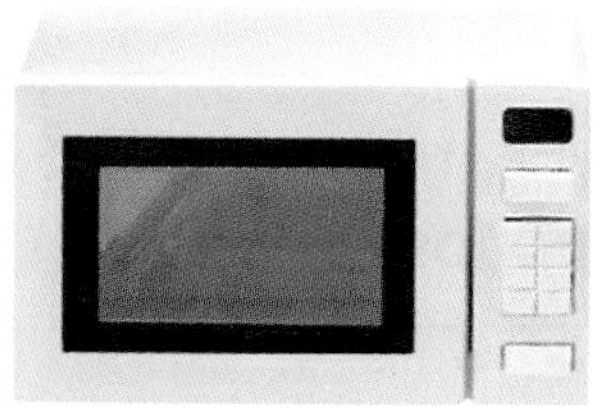

middle

the place that is the same distance away from all the sides of something

This bear is in the middle of the grass.

milk

a white liquid that you can drink. Milk usually comes from cows.

mind
1 be worried or unhappy about something

I don't mind spiders.

2 be careful of something

minute
an amount of time. There are 60 seconds in a minute and 60 minutes in an hour.

It's a few minutes past nine.

mirror
a special piece of glass that you can see yourself in

miss
1 feel unhappy because someone is not with you

Liddy misses her mum.

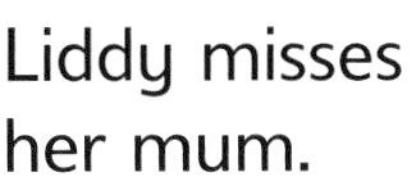

2 not catch a bus or train

mistake
If you make a mistake, you do something wrong.

I made a spelling mistake.

mix
put things together to make one thing

Oliver is mixing flour, sugar, eggs, butter and currants to make cakes.

model
a small copy of something

Billy is playing with his model ship.

money
coins and notes that you use to buy things

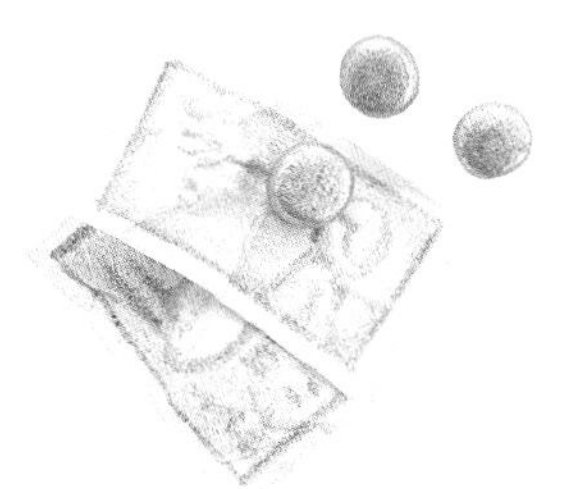

monkey
an animal with a long tail and long arms and legs

month
a part of the year that lasts about 4 weeks. There are 12 months in a year.

January
February
March
April
May
June
July
August
September
October
November
December

Moon
the big, bright thing that you often see in the sky at night

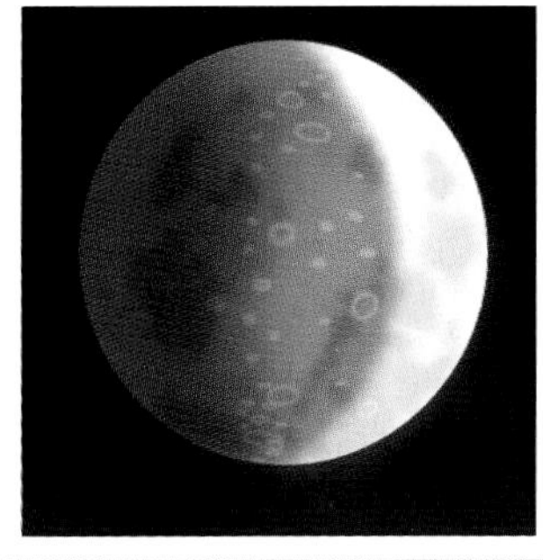

more
a bigger number, amount or size

Sally has more sand than Amy.

morning
the part of the day before 12 o'clock (midday)

most
the biggest number or amount

Which caterpillar has the most black stripes?

moth
an insect with four large wings

motorbike
a big, heavy bicycle with an engine

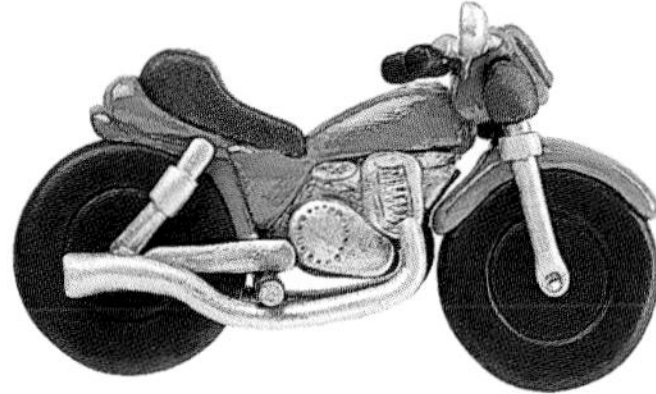

mountain
a very high piece of land. Mountains are taller than hills.

mouse
1 (plural: mice) a small, furry animal with a long tail

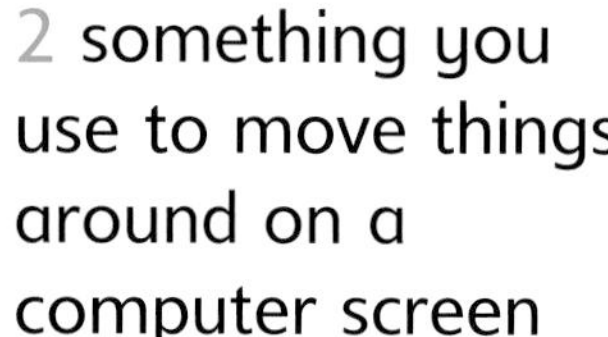

2 something you use to move things around on a computer screen

mouth
the part of your face that you use to eat and talk

move
1 go from one place to another
2 take something from one place to another

The crane is moving the box.

much (more most)
a big amount

Mrs. Moon doesn't have much shopping.

mud
wet earth

Sally is covered in mud.

mushroom
a kind of plant that is the shape of a small umbrella. You can eat some kinds of mushrooms.

music
the sounds that you make when you sing or play a musical instrument

Nn nail *to* nest

nail
1 a pointed thing that you use to join pieces of wood together

2 one of the hard parts at the end of your fingers and toes

name
what you call a person or thing

narrow
If something is narrow, its sides or edges are not far apart.

The gap is too narrow for the the kitten to get through.

nature
everything in the world, such as plants and animals, not made by people

naughty
If you are naughty, you do things that you are not meant to do.

Naughty Pip has stolen Jack's cake.

near
not far away; close

The school is near the river.

neck
the part of your body that joins your head to your shoulders

A giraffe has a very long neck.

necklace
something pretty that you wear around your neck

need
If you need something, you must have it.

Sam needs a sleep.

needle
1 a thin, pointed piece of metal that you use for sewing

2 a long metal or plastic stick that you use for knitting

neighbour
someone who lives near you

The people who live in these two houses are neighbours.

nest
a home made by birds and some other animals. Birds lay their eggs in nests.

net[1]

1 a kind of bag that you use to catch fish and other animals

2 the thing you hit balls over in games such as tennis

Net[2]

a short name for the Internet

Polly is using the Net.

never

not at any time

The grumpy postman never smiles.

new

1 just made, bought or born

Julia has new shoes.

2 different

a new school

news

information about things that have happened in your life or in the world

Mrs. Beef has some sad news.

newspaper

big sheets of paper with stories and pictures about the news

next

1 the one after this

2 nearest to; beside

The red car is next to a yellow car.

nice

If you think something is nice, you like it.

Danny has made a nice picture.

night

the time when it is dark outside and people sleep

nod

move your head up and down

The dog is nodding.

noise

a sound that someone or something makes

The baby is making lots of noise.

noisy

very loud

The boys are being very noisy.

nose

the part of your face that you use to smell and breathe

now

at this time

The clown takes a pie out of his bag...

...now he trips.

ocean

a very large sea

note

1 a sound that you make when you sing or play music

a high note

2 a short message that you write

3 a piece of paper money

number

a word or sign that shows how many

1 7 88 1,200

three twenty-two

one hundred

o'clock

a word you use when you say what time it is

It's seven o'clock.

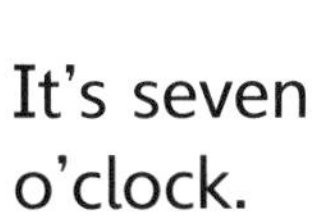

notebook

a book with clean pages for you to write on

nurse

someone who looks after people who are ill or hurt

octopus

a sea animal with eight long arms

notice

see something and pay attention to it

Annie hasn't noticed the clown.

nut

something with a hard shell. Many kinds of nuts are good to eat.

odd

1 An odd number is a number that you can't divide by two.

The bunny is jumping on odd numbers.

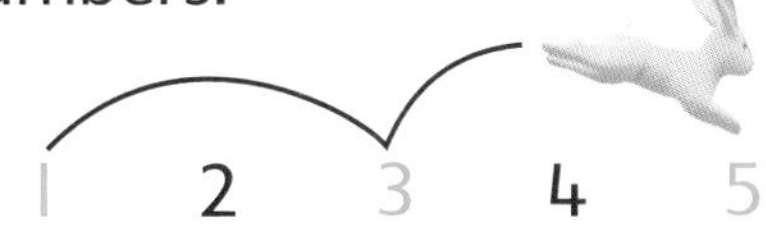

2 strange or unusual

often to other

often
If you do something often, you do it a lot.

Mr. Dot and Jack often do the shopping.

oil
a thick liquid. Some oil is used to make machines work or to make heat. Some oil from plants is used for cooking.

cooking oil

old
1 If someone or something is old, they have lived for a long time.

2 made or bought some time ago

an old shoe

once
1 only one time

We went up in a balloon once.

2 after; as soon as

You can watch TV once you've done your homework.

onion
a round vegetable with papery skin and a strong smell and taste

only
and no more; just

Becky only has two strawberries.

open[1]
1 move something such as a door so that you can go through it

2 take the lid off something

Mrs. Dot is opening the box.

open[2]
If something is open, you can go through it or into it.

The pet shop is open all day.

opposite[1]
The opposite of something is the thing that is the most different from it.

Big is the opposite of small.

opposite[2]
If two things or people are opposite each other, they are facing each other.

Becky is sitting opposite the teddy.

orange

1 a round, juicy fruit with a thick skin

2 a colour

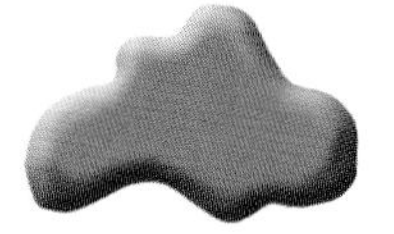

other
1 different

2 one of two
Where's your other shoe?

outside

1 not inside a building

Let's go outside!

2 not in something

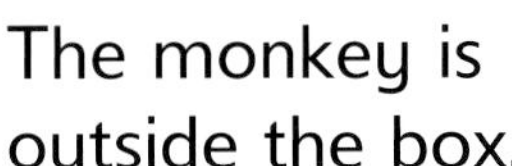

The monkey is outside the box.

over

1 on top of

The bird is flying over the tree.

2 above or across
3 finished
4 down

owl

a bird with big eyes. Owls catch small animals at night.

own

If you own something, it is yours.

Mrs. Bird owns a pet shop.

page

a piece of paper in a book

Turn the page.

paint[1]

a special liquid that you use to put colour on things

bottles of paint

paint[2]

1 use a brush and paints to make a picture

2 put paint on something to change its colour

pair

the name for two things that go together

a pair of socks

palace

a very large house where kings, queens, princes and princesses live

pale

If a colour is pale, it is very light.

pale blue

pale green

pale yellow

paper

1 something that you write, draw and paint on

2 short for newspaper

parachute

a large piece of cloth that can carry people safely to the ground from a plane

parent
a mother or father

Mr. and Mrs. Dot are Polly and Jack's parents.

park[1]
a big piece of land where people can walk and play

park[2]
leave a car somewhere

Jan and Jo are going to park in the car park.

parrot
a bird with bright feathers and a curved beak

part
something that belongs to something bigger

A wheel is part of a car.

party
when a group of friends meet to eat, drink and have fun together

a fancy dress party

pass
1 go past someone or something

passing the bank

2 give something to someone when they can't reach it

3 do well in a test or exam

past[1]
the time that has gone

This is how some people dressed in the past.

past[2]
by or beside

The children and dogs are running past the pet shop.

path
a small road for people to walk or ride on

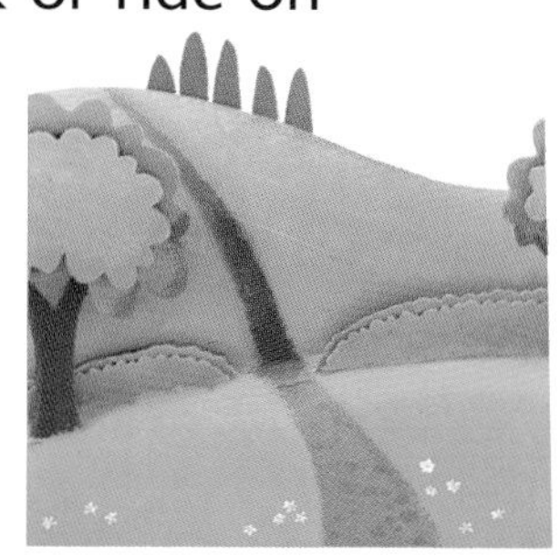

paw
an animal's foot

a tiger's paw

pay
give someone money for something

Ethan is paying for an apple.

pea
a very small, green, round vegetable

peach
a soft, round fruit with a furry skin

peak
1 the very top of a mountain

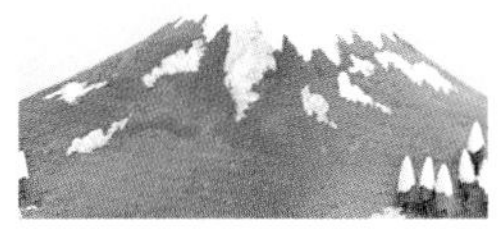

2 the round, front part of a cap

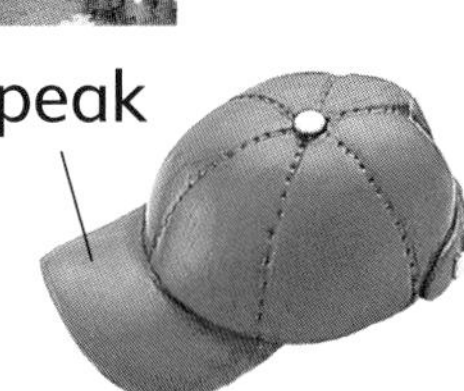

peanut
a small, oval nut. Peanuts are often roasted before you eat them.

pear

a juicy green or yellow fruit

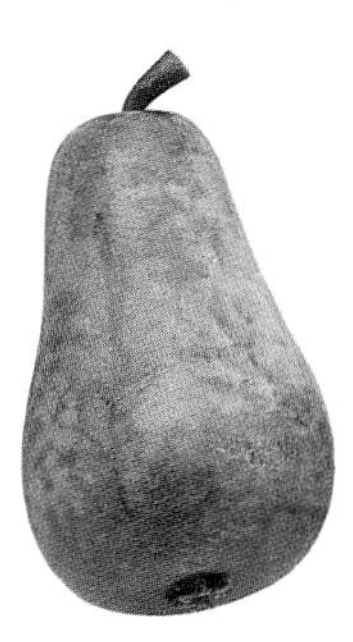

pebble
a smooth, round stone. You find pebbles on beaches.

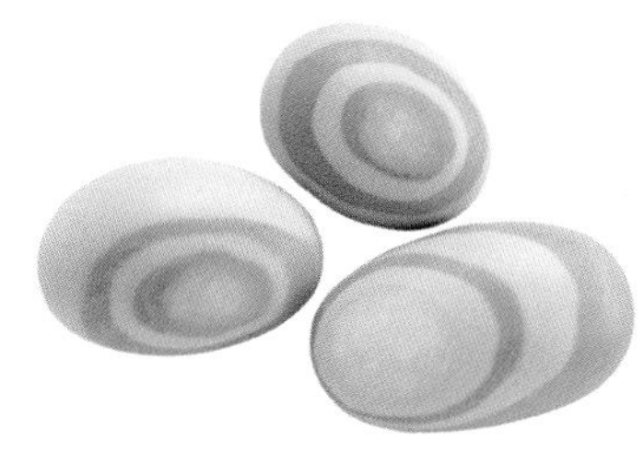

pen
a metal or plastic thing that you use to write or draw in ink

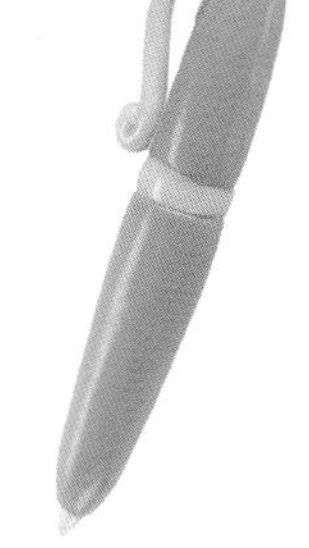

pencil
a long, thin piece of wood with a black stick in the middle that you use for writing and drawing

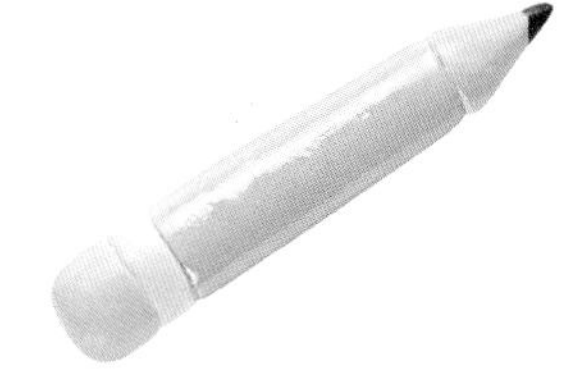

penguin
a black and white bird that lives in cold places

people
men, women and children

There are seven people here.

pepper
1 a black or grey powder you can put on food to add flavour.

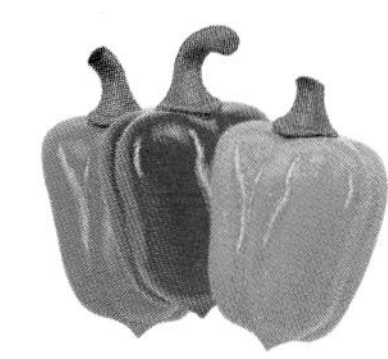

2 a type of vegetable

person
a man, woman or child

This person is a builder.

pet
an animal that you keep at home

phone (short for telephone)
something you use to talk to someone in another place

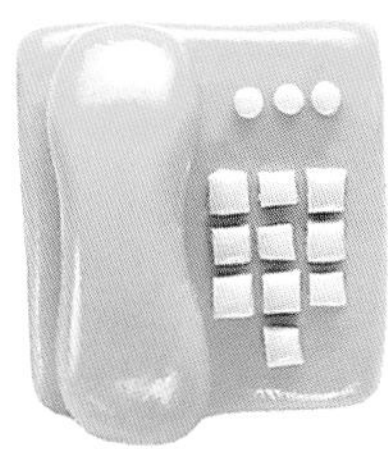

photograph
a picture that you take with a camera

Polly is looking at photographs.

piano
a musical instrument with black and white keys that you tap with your fingers

pick
1 choose something

2 take fruit or flowers from a tree or plant

picnic
a meal that you take to eat outdoors

picture
a painting, drawing or photograph

piece
a part of something

pillow
something that you rest your head on when you are lying in bed

pilot
someone who flies a plane

Jim wants to be a pilot when he grows up.

pineapple
a large yellow or brown fruit, with pointed leaves at the top

pizza
a flat, round piece of bread with tomatoes, cheese and other food on top

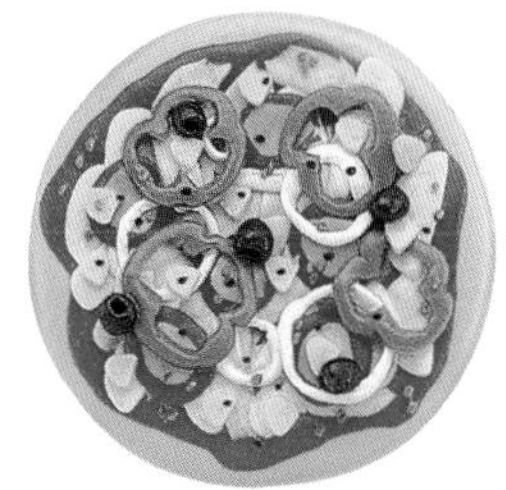

place

somewhere such as a building, country or town. It can be very big or small.

a good place for a snack

plan[1]

a map of a building or a place

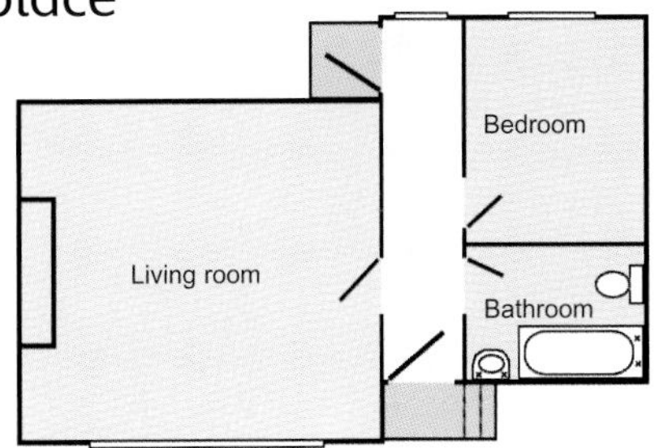

plan[2]

decide how to do something

Mrs. Dot is planning a party.

plane (short for aeroplane)

a big machine that flies

planet

an enormous, round thing that goes around the Sun. The Earth is a planet.

plant

a living thing that grows in soil or in water. Trees and flowers are plants.

plate

a round, flat thing that you put food on

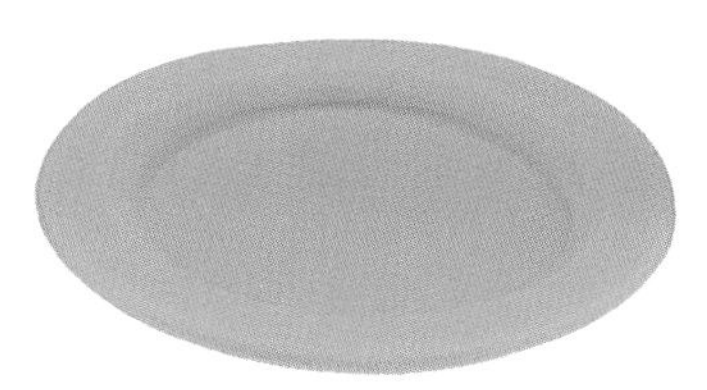

play

1 do something for fun

2 use a musical instrument to make music

3 take part in a sport

playground

a place where you can play outdoors

please

a word that you say when you ask for something in a polite way

plum

a small, soft fruit with red, purple or yellow skin

pocket

a small bag that is part of your clothes. You can keep things in your pockets.

Renata is putting her hands in her pockets.

poem
a piece of writing. Poems usually have short lines and may have words that rhyme.

police car

a special car that the police use for their work

poor
1 If you are poor, you don't have much money.

2 a word you use when you feel sorry for someone

Poor Ross, his tummy hurts.

point[1]
1 the sharp end of something

the point of a pencil

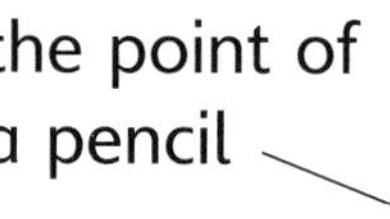

2 part of the score in a game

I have three points now.

pond
a small area of water

potato
a white, red or brown vegetable that grows under the ground

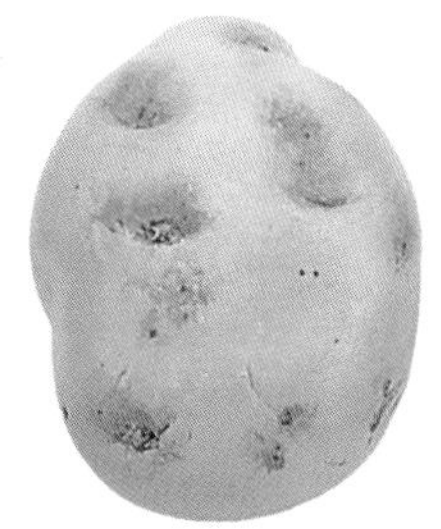

point[2]
use your finger to show where something is

Polly is pointing to Jack's nose.

pony
a small horse

present
something special that you give to someone or that they give to you

police
The police are people whose job is to stop people from breaking the law.

pool
a place where people go to swim or play in water

press
push something

Danny is pressing down the blue paper to make the sea.

pretend *to* puppet

pretend
act as if something is true when it is not

pretending to be asleep

pretty
nice to look at

Anya is wearing a pretty red dress.

price
how much money something costs

prince
the son of a king or queen

princess
the daughter of a king or queen or the wife of a prince

prize
something that you win when you do well

promise
say that you will really do something

puddle
a small pool of water on the ground that you see after it has been raining

pull
move someone or something towards you

Jack is pulling the big parcel.

pumpkin
a very big, round fruit with a hard orange or yellow skin

pupil
someone who is learning something, usually in a school

a photo of Mr. Levy and some of his pupils

puppet
a kind of doll that you make move

Qq quack to quiz

puppy
a young dog

a puppy and a dog

push
move someone or something away from you

Thomas is pushing the big parcel.

put (put put)
move something to a place

Oliver is putting a bottle of green paint on the table.

puzzle
a game that you have to think about very carefully

quack
When a duck quacks, it opens its beak and makes a loud sound.

quarter
one of four pieces of something that are the same size

a quarter

queen
a woman who rules a country. Queens are not chosen.

Joy is dressed up as a queen.

question
what you say or write when you want to find out something

quick
1 If someone or something is quick, they move very fast.

2 lasting only a short time

quiet
not making much noise

You need to be very quiet to creep up on someone.

quite
1 fairly or rather

I'm quite tired.

2 completely

Mr. Bun hasn't quite finished all his baking.

quiz
a kind of game where you have to answer questions

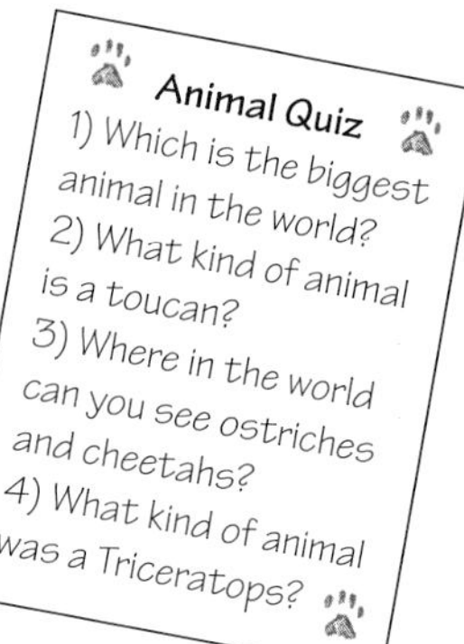

Rr rabbit to real

rabbit
a furry animal with long ears and a short tail

race
a competition to find out who is the fastest

radio
a machine that plays music and programmes that you can listen to

rain
If it rains, drops of water fall down from the sky.

rainbow
a curved band of different colours that you sometimes see in the sky

raisin
a small, dried grape that you can eat as a snack or in cakes

raspberry
a small, soft, red fruit

rat
a small animal with a long tail and sharp teeth

reach
1 stretch out your hand to touch something

The firefighter is reaching out to rescue the cat.

2 arrive at a place

read (read read)
look at words and understand what they mean

ready
If you are ready, you can do something immediately.

These children are ready to go swimming.

real
1 not a copy

Is that fruit real or plastic?

2 true

I like real adventure stories.

recorder
a musical instrument that you blow into

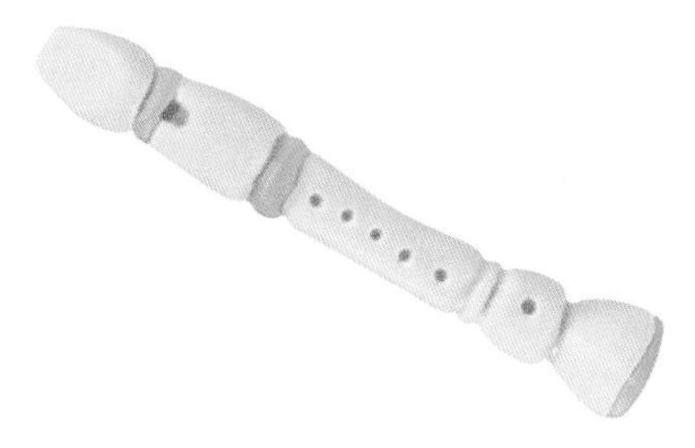

refrigerator
(also called a fridge)
a kind of metal cupboard that keeps food cold

remember
bring something into your mind again

Fiona can remember the order of the colours of the rainbow.

reply
give an answer

Minnie is replying to her dad's question.

rescue
help someone or something escape from danger

rhinoceros
(also called a rhino)
a very big animal with thick skin and horns on its nose

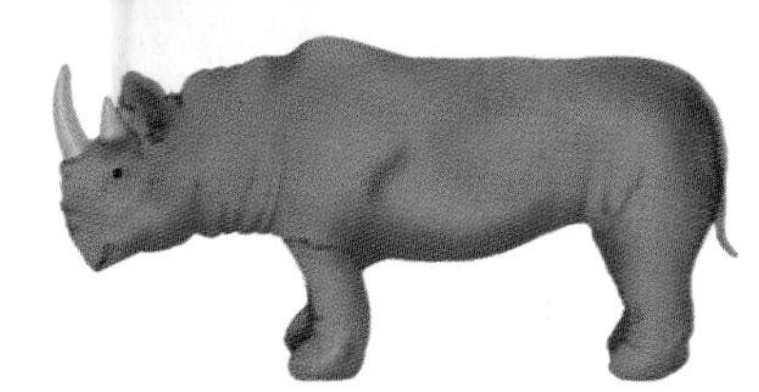

ribbon
a long, thin piece of cloth that you tie around things

Becky has green ribbons in her hair.

rice
a food that comes from a kind of grass plant. You cook and eat grains of rice.

rich
If you are rich, you have a lot of money.

a rich popstar

ride (rode ridden)
sit on a bicycle or horse and move along

right
1 without any mistakes in it

That's the right answer.

2 the side opposite the left side

The puppet is on Greta's right hand.

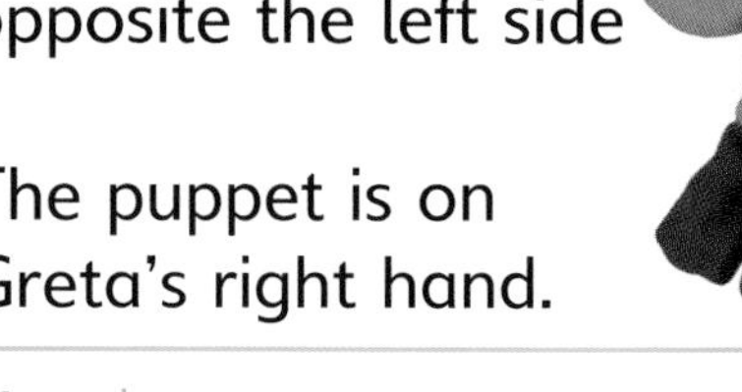

ring[1]
1 something pretty that you wear around your finger

2 a circle with a hole in the middle

ring *to* round

ring[2] (rang rung)
When a bell or telephone rings, it makes a loud noise.

The phone's ringing.

ripe
If fruit is ripe, it is soft and ready to eat.

river
a wide line of water that flows across land to the sea

These houses are near the river.

road
a hard piece of ground that goes from one place to another

robot
a machine that can do some of the things that people do

a toy robot

rock
1 a very big stone

2 a kind of music with a strong beat

Steve likes to play rock.

rocket
a machine that takes astronauts into space. Rockets travel very fast.

a toy rocket

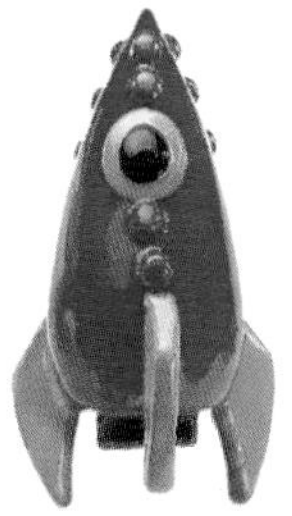

roof
the part of a building that keeps the rain out

room
1 a space inside a building with walls around it

This plan shows six rooms.

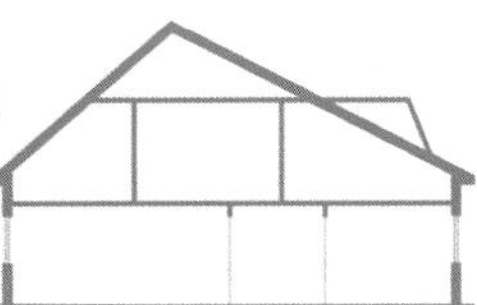

2 space

Is there any room for me?

rope
something made of lots of strong threads twisted together. You can use a rope for pulling heavy things.

rose
a flower with a prickly stem. Many roses smell nice.

round
shaped like a circle or ball

Drums are usually round.

rug
something that covers part of a floor

ruler
a flat piece of plastic, wood or metal that you use to measure things and draw straight lines.

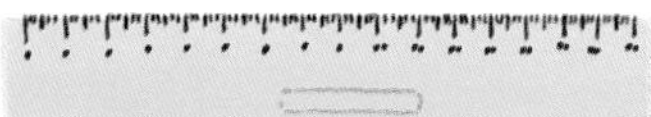

run (ran run)
move quickly using your legs

rush
do something quickly; hurry

Jack, Polly and the dogs are rushing past the post office.

sad
not happy

saddle
a seat for a rider on a bicycle or horse

safe
1 If you are safe, you are not in danger.
2 If something is safe, it can't hurt you.

a safe place to cross

sailor
someone who works on a ship

salad
a mixture of uncooked food, such as lettuce and tomatoes

salami
a kind of big sausage with a strong flavour. You usually eat thin slices of salami.

salt
a white powder that you put on food or use in cooking to add flavour

same
If two things or people are the same, they are just like each other.

The twins always wear the same clothes.

sand *to* scooter

sand
a powder made of tiny bits of rock and shell. It covers some beaches and deserts.

sandal
a kind of shoe that you wear when it is hot

sandwich
two pieces of bread with another kind of food between them

saucer
a small plate that you put under a cup

a cup and saucer

sausage
something that you eat made from chopped meat put into a special skin

save
1 rescue someone or something from danger

2 keep money to spend later

Jack saves coins in this cow money box.

saw
a tool that you use to cut wood

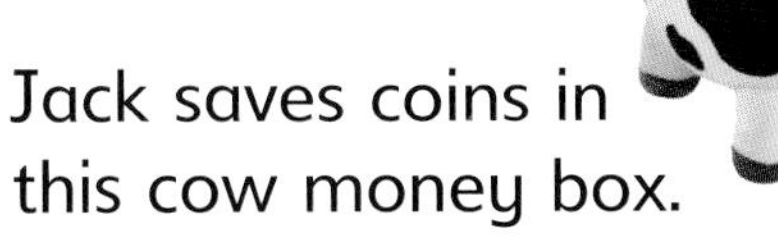

say (said said)
speak words

scarf
a long thing that you wear around your neck to keep warm

school
a place where children go to learn

scissors
something you use to cut paper or cloth

scooter
a small machine that you can push along with one foot

sea
a very large area of salty water

seal
an animal with smooth fur that lives in the sea and on land

search
look carefully for something

Annie, Megan and Tim are searching for their friend.

seat
a place where you can sit

secret
something that only a few people know

Amy is telling Anna a secret.

see (saw seen)
1 use your eyes to look at something

Can you see the clown?

2 meet someone

I'll see you on Monday.

sell (sold sold)
let someone have something if they give you money

Mrs. Hussain is selling Ethan an apple.

send (sent sent)
make something or someone go somewhere

Jack is sending a letter to his friend.

sentence
a group of words that makes sense. A sentence starts with a capital letter and ends with a full stop.

My dad likes apples.

a sentence

sew (sewed sewn)
join pieces of cloth together using a needle and thread

shadow
a dark shape that is made by something getting in the way of light

shake (shook shaken)
move something up and down or from side to side

Anton loves to shake his rattle.

shallow to shoe

shallow
not going down very far; not very deep

The paddling pool is shallow.

shampoo
a liquid that you use when you wash your hair

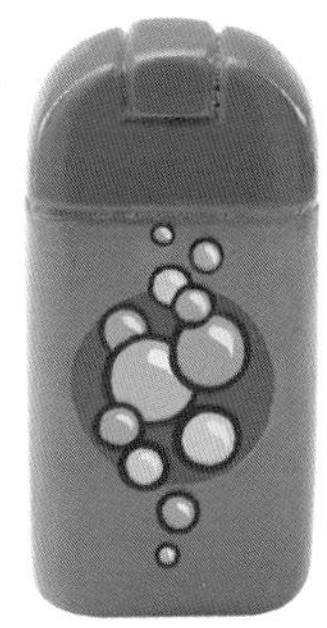

share
let someone have a part of something or use something with you

Bill is sharing his cherries with Ben.

shark
a big fish with sharp teeth

sharp
If something is sharp, it has a very thin edge or a point that can cut or prick you.

a sharp pencil

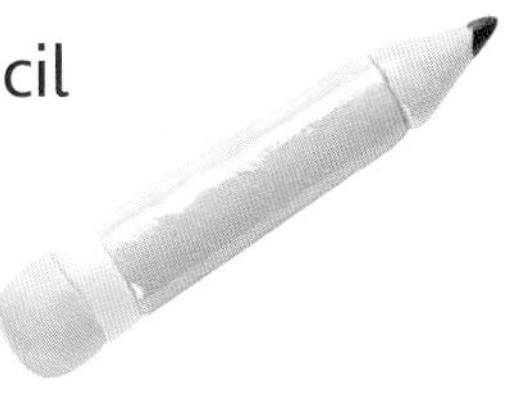

sheep (sheep)
a farm animal with a woolly coat. Most wool comes from sheep.

sheet
1 a big piece of cloth that you put on a bed

2 a flat piece of paper, glass or plastic

shelf (shelves)
a long, flat piece of wood, metal or plastic that is fixed to a wall

shell
1 the hard cover around some sea animals and snails

2 the hard part around eggs and nuts

ship
a very big boat that carries people and things over the sea

shirt
something that you wear on the top part of your body. A shirt often has buttons down the front.

shoe
something you wear to cover your foot

short
1 not very long

Maisie has short hair.

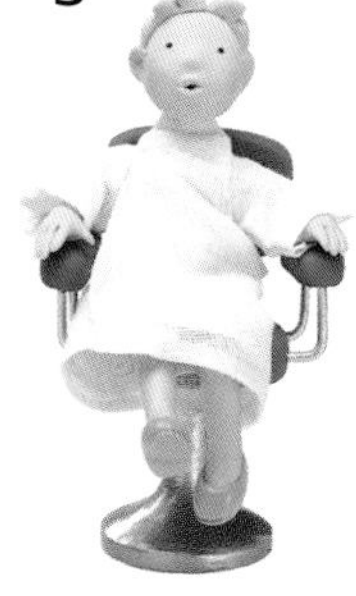

2 not tall

Minnie is short for her age.

shorts
trousers with short legs

shoulder
a part of your body between your neck and your arm

Jack's shoulder

shout
talk very loudly

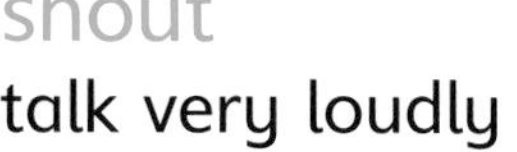

show (showed shown)
1 let someone see something

Jack is showing Thomas his hands.

2 explain how to do something by doing it yourself

shower
1 something you use to wash yourself

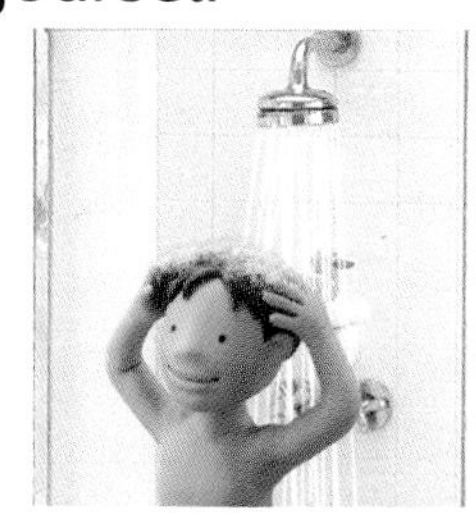

2 a short fall of rain

shrink (shrank shrunk)
get smaller

This pink cardigan shrank in the wash.

shut (shut shut)
move a door or cover to block a space or opening; close

Danny is shutting the door of the playhouse.

side
1 the edge of something

2 a flat surface of something

A piece of paper has two sides.

3 a team

sign[1]
1 words or pictures that tell you what to do

a road sign

2 a shape that means something

@ is the sign for "at".

sign[2]
write your name on something

Sign here please.

since
from that time

They've been waiting for the bus since 2.30.

sing to sleeve

sing (sang sung)
use your voice to make music

sink[1]
something that you wash things in. Sinks have taps and a plug.

sink[2] (sank sunk)
go downwards under water

sit (sat sat)
put your bottom on something and rest

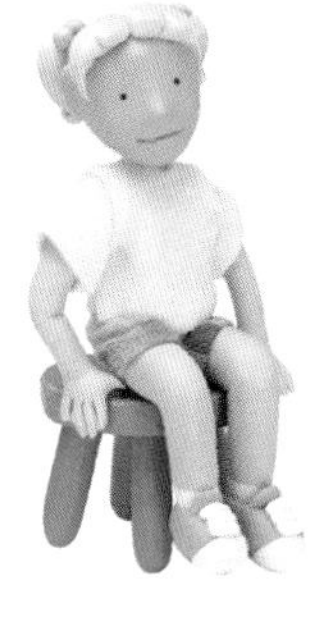

size
how big or small something is

skate
move smoothly on ice wearing special boots called skates

ski
travel on snow wearing two long things called skis on your feet

skin
1 the cover of your body

Babies have smooth skin.

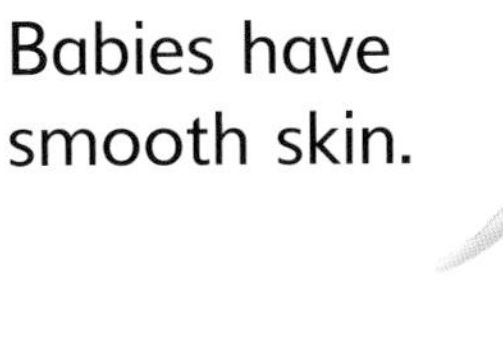

2 the outside layer of a fruit or vegetable

skirt
something that girls and women wear

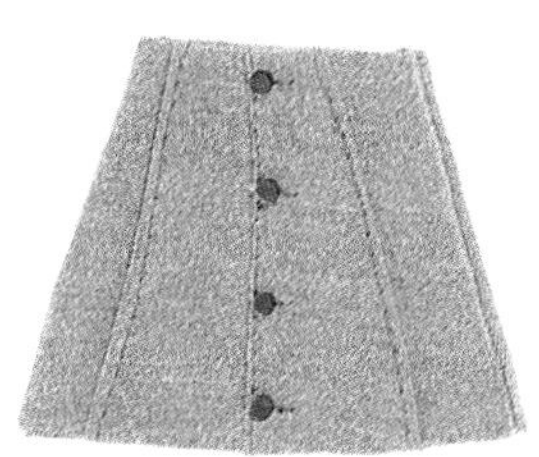

sky
the space above the ground where you can see clouds, stars and planes

sleep (slept slept)
close your eyes and rest your whole body, usually at night

sleeve
a part of a shirt, top, coat, or sweater that covers your arms

slice
a piece of food that has been cut from a larger piece

slide[1]
something you can play on in a playground.

slide[2] (slid slid)
move smoothly over or down something

slip
slide and fall over

slipper
a soft shoe that you wear indoors

slow
If someone or something is slow, they take a long time to go somewhere or do something; not fast

a slow train

slowly
If you do something slowly, it takes a long time.

Sally is riding slowly so that she doesn't spill any sand.

slug
a small, soft animal with no legs, like a snail without a shell

small
not big, large or tall; little

Asha is a small child.

smell (smelt smelt)
1 use your nose to sense something

2 If something smells, you can sense it with your nose.

Your cat smells horrible!

smile
turn up the corners of your mouth to show that you are happy

smooth
If something is smooth, it does not have bumps or lumps in it.

The roller is making the road smooth.

snail
a small, soft animal with no legs and a shell on its back

snake
a long, thin animal with no legs. Some snakes have a poisonous bite.

snow
small, white pieces of ice that fall from the sky when it is very cold

soap
something you use to wash yourself

soccer
(also called football)
a game where two teams try to kick a ball into a net

sock
something you wear on your foot under your shoe

sofa
a long, soft chair for two or more people

soft
not hard or firm

This cat has soft fur.

soil
the earth that plants grow in

soldier
someone whose job is to fight

song
a piece of music with words that you sing

Natalie is singing a song.

soon
happening not long from now

It will soon be 2 o'clock.

sort
a kind or type

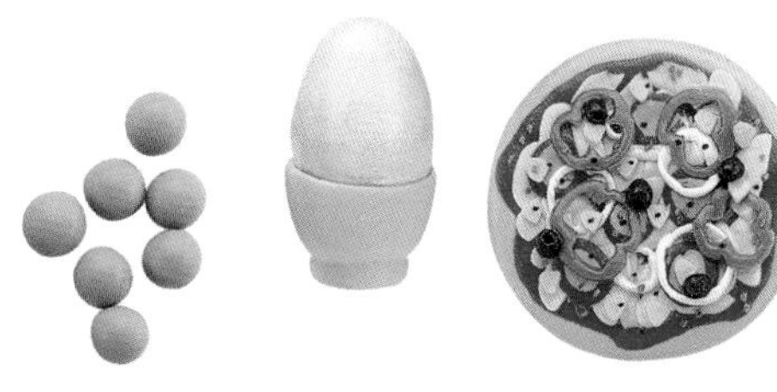

different sorts of food

sound
something that you hear

Parrots make a squawking sound.

soup
a liquid food made from meat or vegetables and water

space
1 an empty place or area

2 everything outside the Earth, including the stars and planets

spacecraft
something that travels into space from the Earth

speak (spoke spoken)
say something

special
1 important or better than usual

2 made for a particular job

Electricians need special tools.

spell[1]
In stories, a spell is special words or a recipe that makes things change or happen.

spell[2] (spelt spelt)
write or say the letters of a word in the right order

spend (spent spent)
use money to buy things

Danny is thinking about how to spend his money.

spider
a small animal with eight legs

spill (spilt spilt)
let liquid fall out of a container by mistake

spinach to star

spinach
a vegetable with dark green leaves

splash
throw liquid around

sponge
something you can use for cleaning things or soaking up liquid

spoon
something you use for stirring things and for eating

sport
a kind of game that you play to get exercise and have fun

spot[1]
1 a small, roundish mark

a dog with black spots

2 a small lump on your skin

spot[2]
notice something

Can you spot a clown in this picture?

squirrel
a small animal with a big, furry tail

stairs
a group of steps inside a building

stamp
a small piece of paper with a picture on it that shows you have paid to post something

stand (stood stood)
be upright on your feet

star
1 a little bright light you can see in the sky at night

2 a shape with points

3 a famous person

a film star

start
do the first part of something; begin

The birds are starting to eat the seeds.

station
a place where people get on or off trains

stay
1 not leave a place

The cows stay in the field all day.

2 live somewhere for a short time

steep
If a hill is steep, it slopes a lot and is hard to climb.

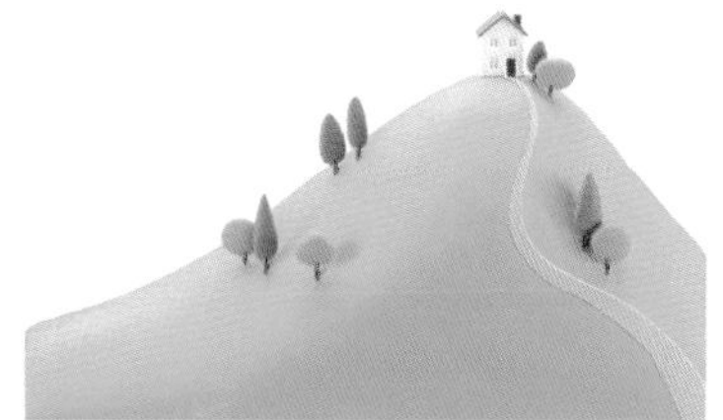

stick[1]
a long, thin piece of wood

stick[2] (stuck stuck)
use glue to join things together

still[1]
If someone or something is still, they are not moving at all.

Milo is standing very still.

still[2]
If something is still happening or is still there, it has not stopped or gone.

Oliver ate one apple...

...but he still has some left.

sting (stung stung)
If an animal or plant stings you, it pricks you and leaves some poison in your body.

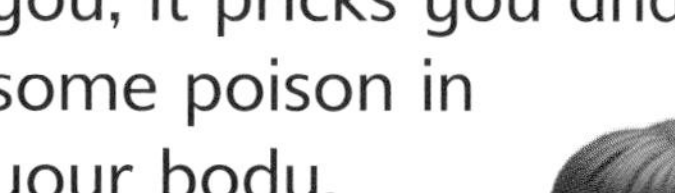

Flora is afraid the bee will sting her.

stir
move something around with a spoon or stick

stone
1 a small piece of rock

2 a hard seed inside fruits such as plums and peaches

stool
a seat without a back

stop

1 not move any more

Jan and Jo stopped at the barrier to take a ticket.

2 not happen any more

storm

a strong wind with lots of rain or snow

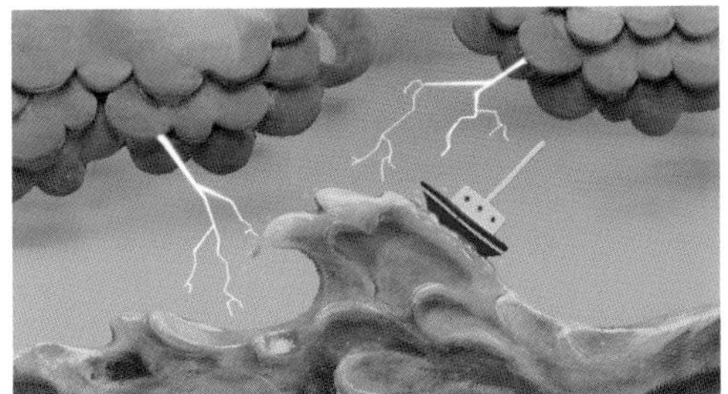

story

words which tell you about something that has happened. A story can be true or made up.

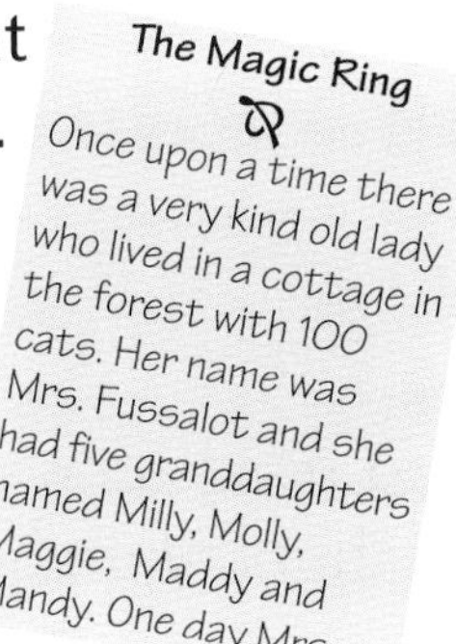
The Magic Ring

Once upon a time there was a very kind old lady who lived in a cottage in the forest with 100 cats. Her name was Mrs. Fussalot and she had five granddaughters named Milly, Molly, Maggie, Maddy and Mandy. One day Mrs.

straight

If something is straight, it does not bend or curve.

Leslie has straight hair.

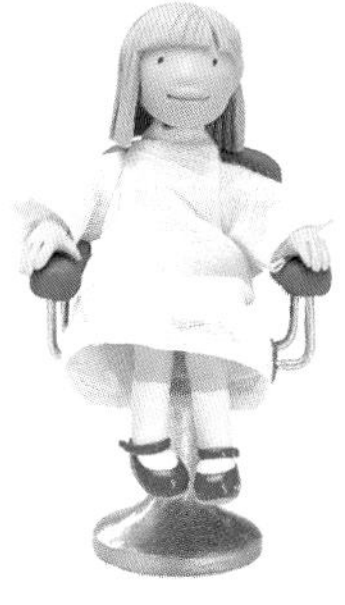

strawberry

a soft, red fruit with tiny seeds on its skin

street

a road in a town or city which usually has buildings on both sides

string

very thin rope that you use to tie things together

strong

1 able to lift heavy things

2 If something is strong, it does not break easily.

3 with a lot of flavour

strong coffee

study[1]

a room for reading, writing or working on a computer

study[2]

learn about something

suddenly

If something happens suddenly, it happens quickly and when you don't expect it.

Suddenly she dropped the vase.

sugar

sweet, white or brown stuff that you can put in drinks or in food

suitcase *to* swim

suitcase
a kind of strong bag for carrying clothes and other things

sum
a maths question using numbers

8 + 2 =

4 – 2 =

10 x 4 =

Sun
the very large, bright thing that you see in the sky in the daytime

sunflower
a very tall flower with yellow petals

sunglasses
something that you can wear on your face to shade your eyes from the Sun

supermarket
a big shop that sells food and other things

sure
If you are sure about something, you know it is true or right.

Dad isn't sure if they've got everything on the list.

surprise
something that you do not expect

It was a surprise when the clown jumped out.

swan
a big white or black bird with a long neck

sweep (swept swept)
use a broom to brush the floor or ground

sweet
1 lovely; cute

a sweet kitten

2 kind

3 If food is sweet, it has the taste of sugar.

swim (swam swum)
move through water using your arms and legs

swimming pool
a place made for people to swim in

swimsuit
special clothes that you wear for swimming

swing[1]
something you can sit on in a playground to go backwards and forwards

swing[2] (swung swung)
move backwards and forwards on something that is hanging

table
a piece of furniture with a flat top and legs

tail
the part at the end of some animals' bodies

take (took taken)
1 move or carry something

Amy is taking sand to the sandpit.

2 steal something

talk
speak to people

tall
If someone or something is tall, their head or top is high above the ground.

taste
put food or drink in your mouth to find out what it's like

taxi
a car that you can pay to ride in

tea
1 a drink made from hot water and dried leaves from a tea plant

a tea bag

2 a meal that you eat in the early evening or afternoon

teacher to thirsty

teacher
someone whose job is to teach other people

team
a group of people who work or play sport together

teddy bear
a soft, furry toy that looks like a bear

telephone
(also called a phone) something you use to talk to someone in another place

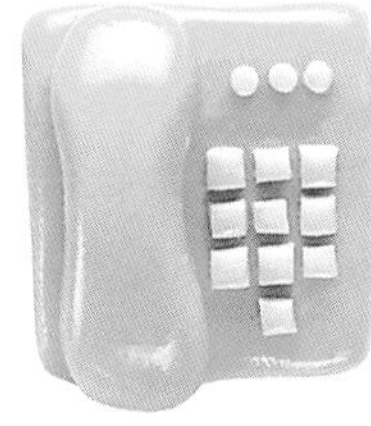

television
(also called a TV) something that shows moving pictures and sends out sounds

tell (told told)
1 talk to someone about something

Mrs. Beef is telling them about her cat.

2 say that someone must do something

tent
a kind of small house made from strong cloth that you can sleep in outside

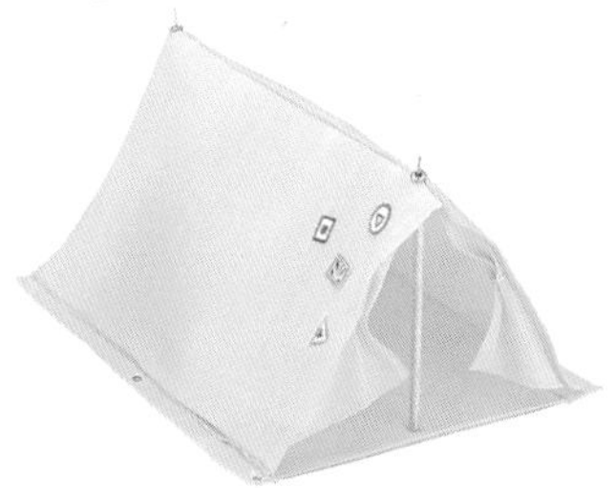

thank
tell someone that you are pleased with something they have done or given you

Polly is thanking Marco for the present.

thin
1 not wide; narrow

2 not weighing much; not fat

a thin cat

thing
anything you can see, touch, do or think about

There are lots of things on the table, but Tina still has a few things to do.

think (thought thought)
1 use your mind

2 believe something

Maddy thinks spiders are scary.

thirsty
If you are thirsty, you want to drink something.

through *to* toe

through
from one side to the other

Mr. Bun went out through the door.

throw (threw thrown)
make something move through the air

Anna is going to throw the ball.

thumb
the shortest of your five fingers, at the side of your hand

ticket
a small piece of paper or card that shows you have paid for something

tie
hold things together with a string, rope or ribbon

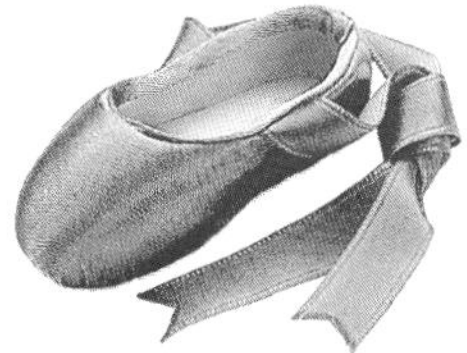

Someone has tied the ribbons together.

tiger
a big, wild animal with orange fur and black stripes

time
1 a moment shown on a clock or watch

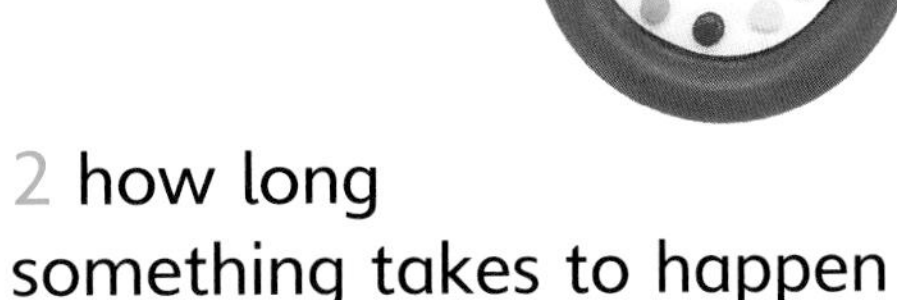

2 how long something takes to happen

tiny
very small

a small cat   a tiny cat

tip
the very end part of something

This fox's tail has a white tip.

toast
a piece of bread which has been cooked until it goes brown

toddler
a young child who is just beginning to walk

toe
one of the five parts on the end of your foot

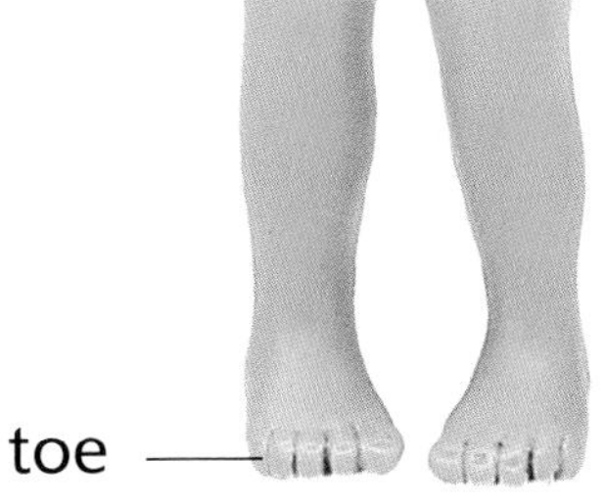

together
with another person or thing

Jenny and Ethan are playing together.

tonight
the night or evening of this day

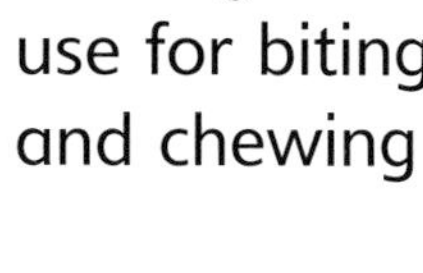

top
1 the highest part of something

The kitten is on the top of the desk.

2 something that you wear on the upper part of your body

toilet
a special bowl with a seat where you go to wee or poo

tooth (teeth)
one of the hard white things inside your mouth that you use for biting and chewing

touch
1 feel something with part of your body

2 If things touch, they are so close there is no space between them.

Please do not touch!

tomato
a soft, juicy red fruit that you eat in salads

toothbrush
a brush that you use for cleaning your teeth

towel
a big piece of thick, soft cloth that you use to dry yourself

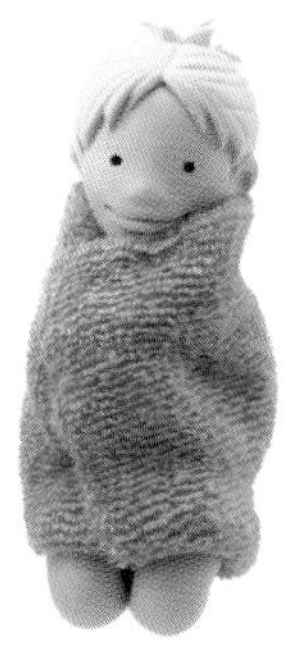

tongue
the long, soft part inside your mouth that you use for tasting, eating and talking

toothpaste
a thick liquid that you put on a toothbrush to clean your teeth

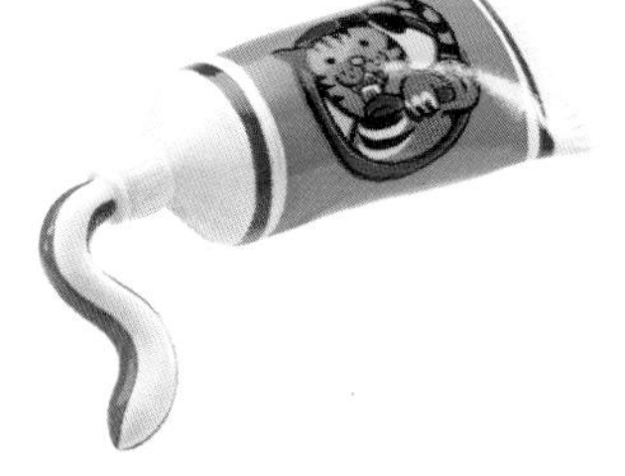

town
a place with lots of roads and buildings where many people live and work

toy

something that you play with

tractor

a big thing with large back wheels. Farmers use tractors to pull other machines or heavy loads.

train

a very big thing that can carry a lot of people along on rails

tree

a very large plant with leaves, branches and a trunk

truck

a big thing with wheels that carries things from one place to another

true

1 correct or right

TRUE OR FALSE?
A. An aardvark is a plant.
B. Penguins can't fly.
C. Tadpoles turn into butterflies.

2 If a story is true, it really happened.

try

1 work hard to do something you want to do

They are trying to move the parcel.

2 test something

T-shirt

something with short sleeves that you wear on the top part of your body

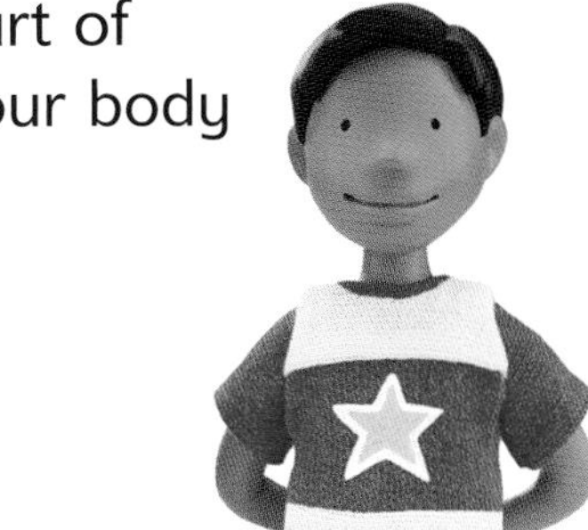

turkey

1 a big bird that farmers keep

2 a kind of meat that comes from a turkey

turn

1 go in a different direction

They are going to turn left.

2 move around

TV

(short for television) something that shows moving pictures and sends out sounds

twin

Twins are two children who have the same mother and were born on the same day. Some twins look alike.

Uu ugly *to* usually

ugly
not pretty to look at

undress
take your clothes off

upside down
with the part that is usually at the top at the bottom

umbrella
something you hold over your head to keep the rain off

unhappy
sad or upset

use
do a job with something

Mr. Clack is using a saw.

under
If something is under something else, it is lower than it.

The kitten is under the planks of wood.

upright
standing straight

useful
If something is useful, it helps you do something.

A wheelbarrow is useful for moving things.

understand (understood understood)
know what something means or how it works

Can you understand what Ben is saying?

upset
not happy; angry

Mrs. Beef is upset because she has lost her cat.

usually
If something usually happens, it nearly always happens.

Sara usually cycles to school.

vacuum cleaner
a machine that you use to clean carpets

vase
something you can put flowers in

vegetable
a plant that you can eat

very
You use the word "very" before another word to make it stronger.

dirty

very dirty

view
what you can see from a particular place

visit
go to see someone or something for a short time

The children are going to visit the museum.

visitor
someone who goes to a place to see someone or something

Polly has some visitors.

voice
the sound you make when you talk, shout or sing

wait
stay in a place until something happens

waiter
a man who brings the food and drink in a café or restaurant

waitress
a woman who brings the food and drink in a café or restaurant

wake (woke woken)
stop sleeping

walk
put one foot in front of the other to move along

wall
1 one side of a room or building

2 something made of stone or brick that divides land

want
If you want something, you need it or would like it.

Jenny wants some more wagons for her train.

warm
1 quite hot

a warm day

2 making you feel quite hot

a warm coat

wash
use soap and water to make someone or something clean

washing machine
a machine that washes clothes

watch[1]
a small clock that you wear on your wrist

watch[2]
look at someone or something to see what happens

water
the clear liquid that falls as rain and comes out of taps

Becky is playing in the water.

wave[1]
a big hill of water in the sea

wave[2]
move your hand from side to side to say hello or goodbye

way
1 how you do something

2 how you get from one place to another

This is the way to the village.

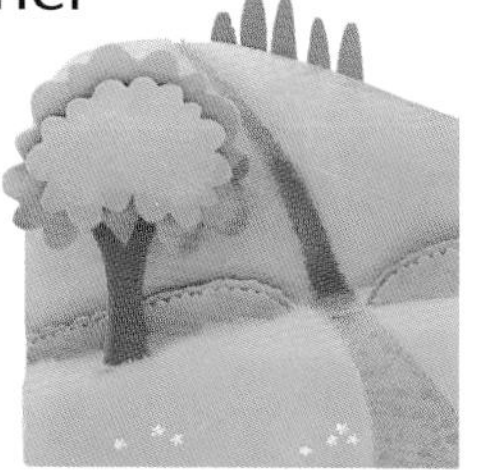

wear (wore worn)
When you wear clothes, they cover your body.

Miriam is wearing a red suit.

weather
what it is like outside, for example windy, rainy, sunny or snowy

cold weather

web
1 A thin net that a spider makes to catch insects.

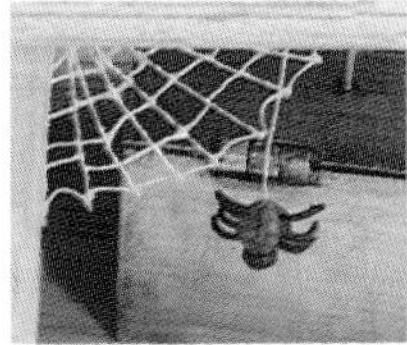

2 Web The part of the Internet that you can use to find out information.

week
A week is seven days. There are 52 weeks in a year.

well
1 If you are well, you are healthy.

2 If you do something well, you are good at it.

Sarah can read very well now.

wet
full of water or covered in water

whale
a very big animal that lives in the sea

wheel
a round thing that can turn around.

while
at the same time as something else is happening

Jack ate a cake while no one was looking.

wide
measuring a lot from one side to the other; not narrow

This sofa is wide enough for three cats.

wild
not looked after by people; not tame

wild animals

win (won won)
come first in a game, race or competition

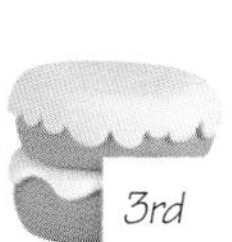

The pink cake won first prize.

wind *to* wrong

wind
air that moves quickly

The wind blew Alison's hat off.

window
something in a wall or in a car that lets in light. There is usually glass in a window.

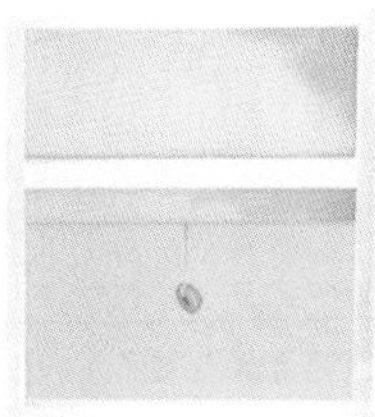

wish
something you want to happen very much

This fairy can give you three wishes.

witch
a woman in a story who can do magic spells

with
1 If you are with someone, you are together.

2 using
Draw with a pencil.

3 that has or who has

a bird with blue feet

woman (women)
a grown-up who is not a man; a lady

wood
1 the hard part of a tree that can be burnt or used to make things

a table made of wood

2 a lot of trees growing together; a small forest

word
a group of sounds or letters that mean something. You use words to speak and write.

a list of words

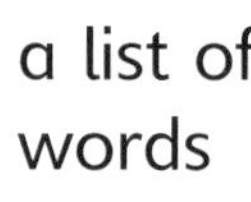

work
1 do a job or something that needs to be done

Mick works as a builder.

2 If something works, it does what it should do.

world
the planet that we live on

write (wrote written)
use a pen or pencil to put letters or words on something

Harry has written his name.

wrong
1 not correct or right

All these answers are wrong.

2 + 3 = 7 X
4 + 6 = 9 X
5 − 3 = 4 X

2 naughty or bad

x

1 You write x after your name to send someone a kiss.

Lots of love from Kathy xxx

2 times or multiplied by

$$2 \times 2 = 4$$

Xmas

a short way of writing "Christmas"

Happy Xmas!

x-ray

a kind of photograph that shows the inside of someone's body

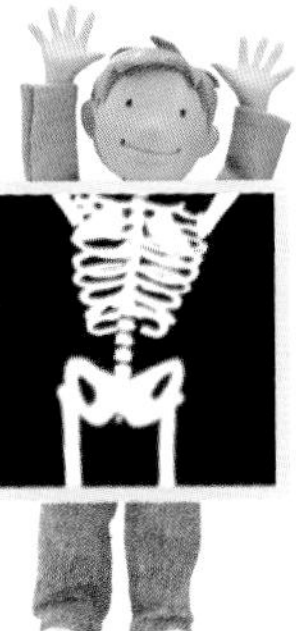

xylophone

a musical instrument with a row of wooden or metal bars. You play it by hitting the bars with special sticks.

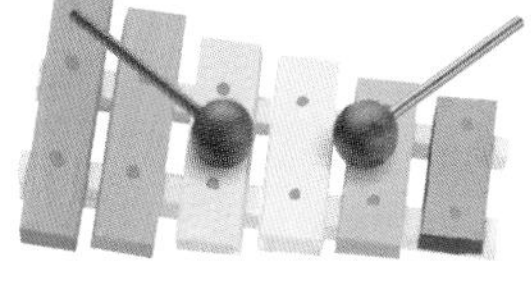

yawn

open your mouth and breathe in deeply because you are tired

year

A year is 12 months.

Freya is five years old. Annie is six years old.

yet

up to this time

Ben can't walk yet.

young

If someone or something is young, they have only lived a short time.

young children

zebra

an animal that looks like a horse with black and white stripes

zero

the name for the number 0; nothing

$$5 - 5 = 0$$

Five take away five equals zero.

zip

something that you use to fasten clothes and bags

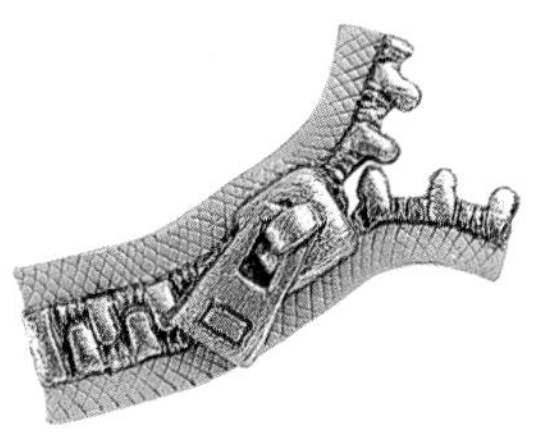

zoo

a place where wild animals are kept so that people can go to see them

We saw a panda at the zoo.

Colours

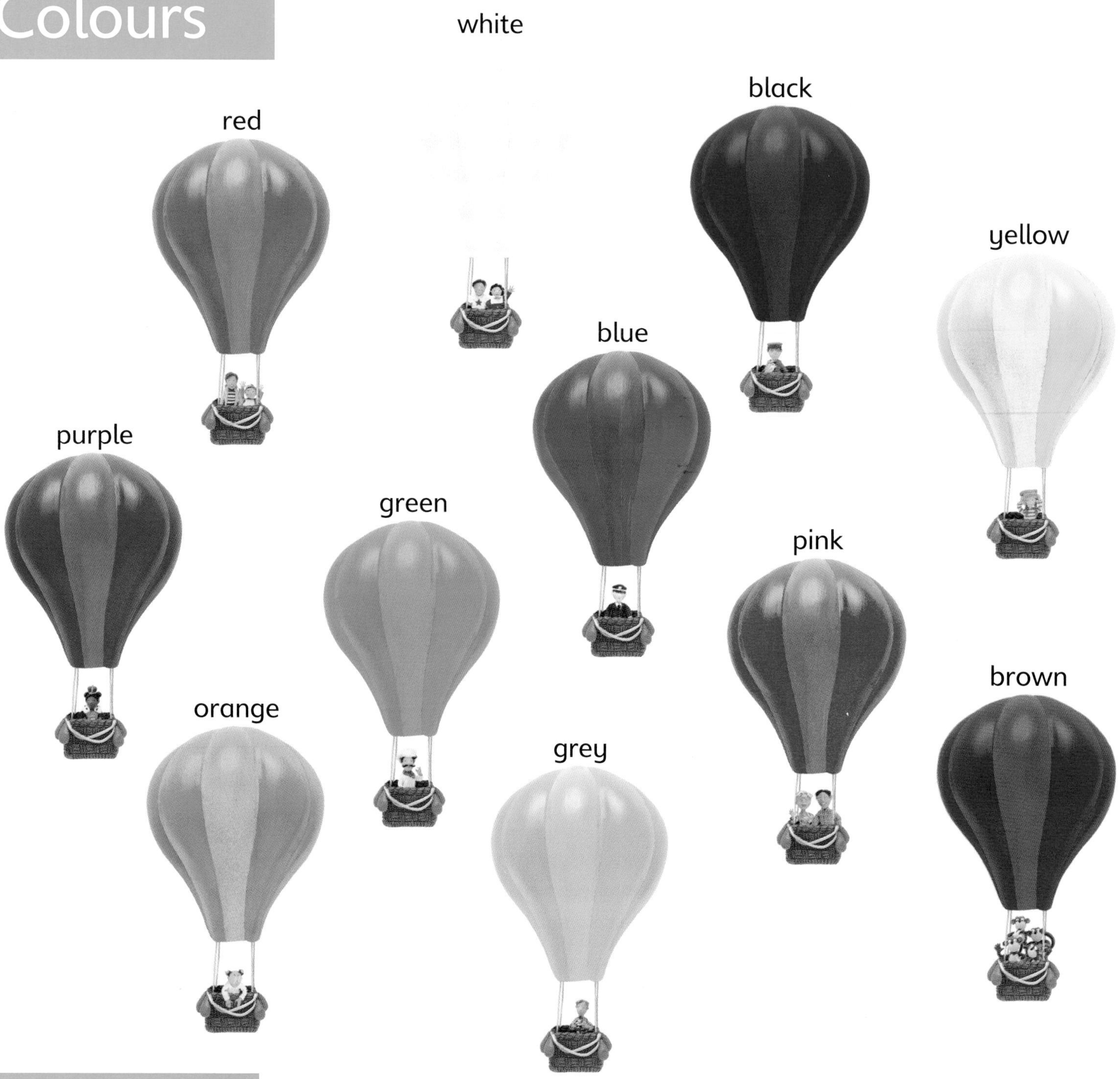

white
red
black
yellow
blue
purple
green
pink
orange
grey
brown

Shapes

square
circle
crescent
oval
triangle
star
rectangle

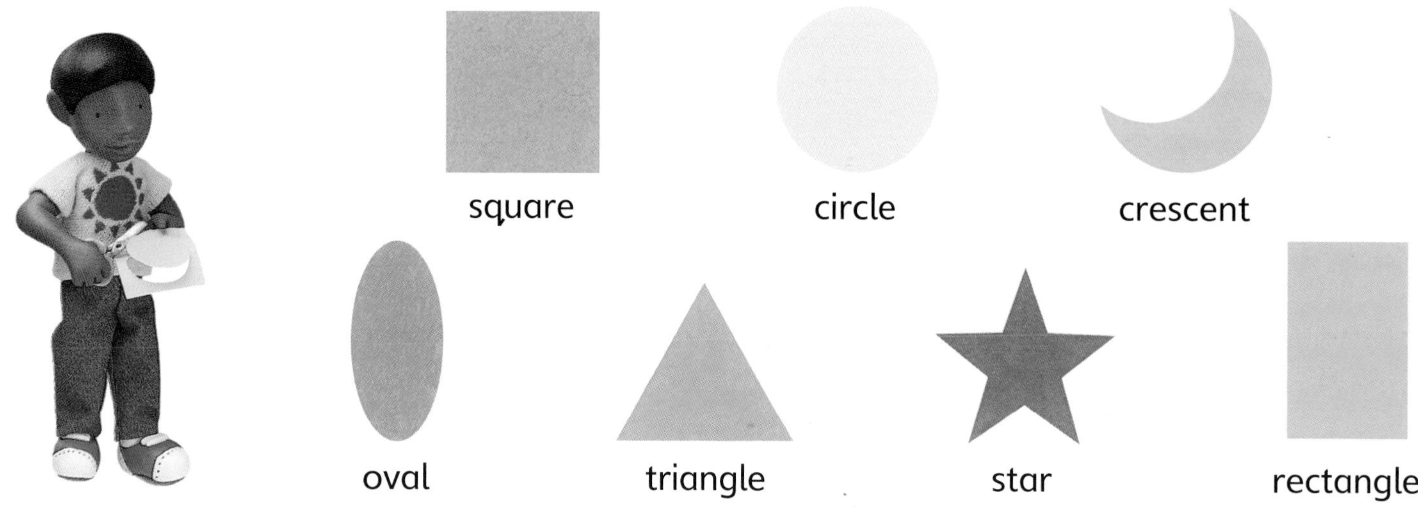

Numbers

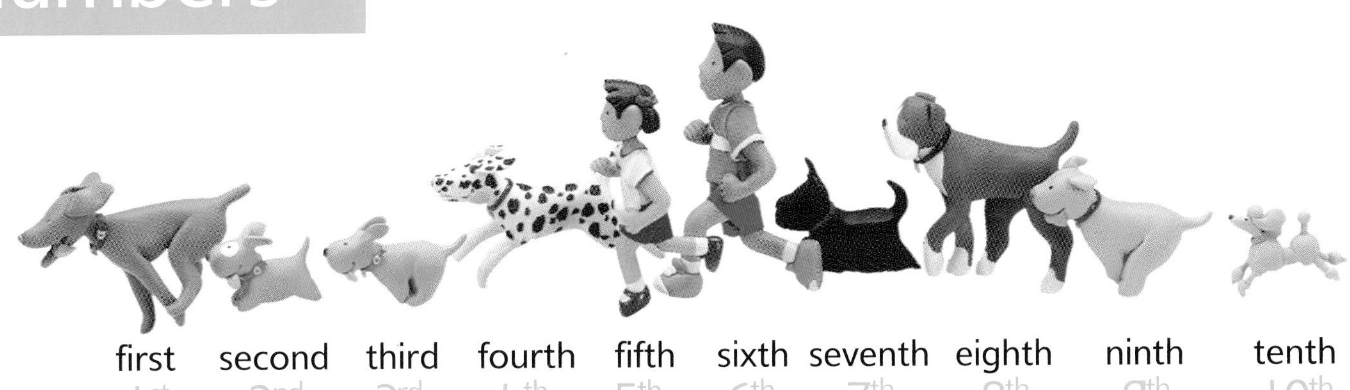

first	second	third	fourth	fifth	sixth	seventh	eighth	ninth	tenth
1st	2nd	3rd	4th	5th	6th	7th	8th	9th	10th

1 one
2 two
3 three
4 four
5 five
6 six
7 seven
8 eight
9 nine
10 ten
11 eleven
12 twelve
13 thirteen
14 fourteen
15 fifteen
16 sixteen
17 seventeen
18 eighteen
19 nineteen
20 twenty

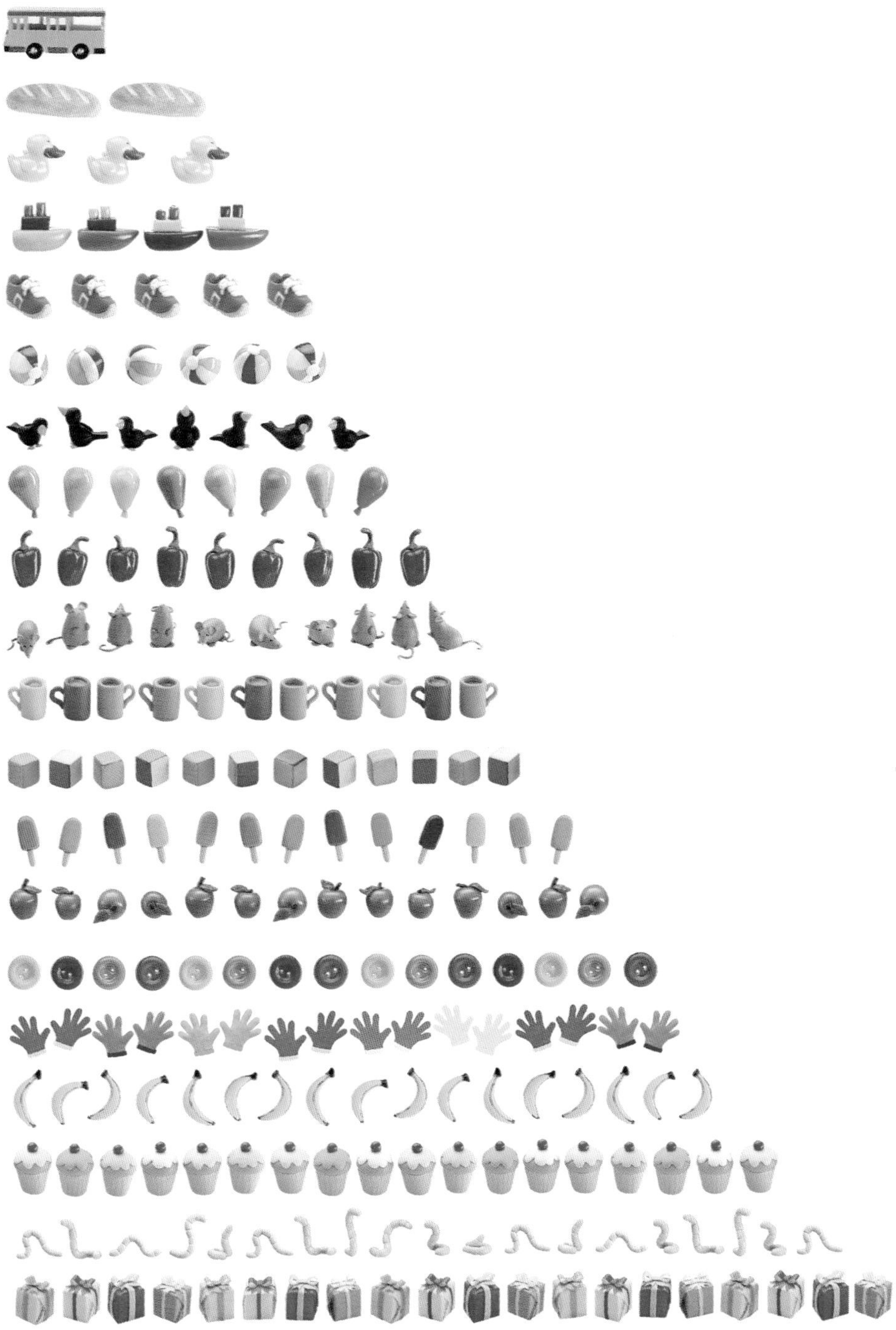

30	40	50	60	70	80	90	100	1000
thirty	forty	fifty	sixty	seventy	eighty	ninety	hundred	thousand

Days and months

Polly's birthday is in January. When is your birthday?

Seasons

Spring

Summer

Autumn

Winter

Family words

Polly is looking at some photographs of her family.

Polly and Jack are sister and brother.

Here are Polly's parents. She calls her mother "Mum" or "Mummy". She calls her father "Dad" or "Daddy".

Jack is his parents' son.

Polly is her parents' daughter.

Here are Polly and Jack with their grandparents. Polly calls her grandmother "Granny". She calls her grandfather "Granddad". What do you call yours?

Here's Daddy with his brother Howard.

Here's Jack when he was a baby.

Howard is Polly's uncle. His wife, Kathy, is Polly's aunt. Their little girl is Polly's cousin Aimee.

Polly and Jack are their parents' children. They are their grandparents' grandchildren. Polly is their granddaughter. Jack is their grandson.

Words we use a lot

a
about
above
across
again
all
almost
also
always
am
among
an
and
another
anybody
anyone
anything
anywhere
apart
are
around
as
at
away

be
because
but
by

can
can't
could
couldn't

each
every
everybody
everyone
everything
everywhere

for
from

get
got

he
he'd
he'll
her
here
hers
herself
he's
him
himself
his
how

I
I'd
if
I'll
I'm
in
into
is
isn't
it
its
it's
itself

just

may
me
might
mine
must
my
myself

no
nobody
none
no one

not
nothing
nowhere

of
off
on
or
our
ours
ourselves
out

she
she'd
she'll
she's
should
so
some
somebody
someone
something
sometimes
somewhere

than
that
the
their
theirs
them
themselves
then
there
these
they
they'd
they'll
they're
this
those
to
today

tomorrow
too

unless
until
up
upon
us

we
we'd
we'll
were
we're
what
when
where
which
who
whose
why
will
won't
would
wouldn't

yes
yesterday
you
you'd
you'll
your
you're
yours
yourself
yourselves

First published in 2002 by Usborne Publishing Ltd,
83-85 Saffron Hill, London EC1N 8RT, England. www.usborne.com

Printed in Italy.

This edition produced for:
The Book People Ltd, Hall Wood Avenue, Haydock, St Helens WA11 9UL